THE SACRED MEANING
OF EVERYDAY WORK

THE
SACRED MEANING OF
EVERYDAY WORK

By Robert H. Tribken

FAITH AND ENTERPRISE PRESS
Sierra Madre, CA 91025

For information about this title or to contact the publisher:
Faith and Enterprise Press
P.O. Box 1098
Sierra Madre, CA 91025
mail@faithandenterprise.org
http://www.faithandenterprise.org

Library of Congress Control Number: Pending
ISBN: 9798986913001

Cover Design: Marc Posch (Opus Creative Group)

The scripture quotations contained herein are from the New Revised Standard Version Bible, © 1989 by the Division of Christian Education of the National Council of the Churches of Christ in the U.S.A. Used by permission. All rights reserved.

Publisher's Cataloging-In-Publication Data:
Names: Tribken, Robert, author.
Title: The sacred meaning of everyday work / by Robert Tribken.
Description: Sierra Madre, CA: Faith and Enterprise Press, 2022. |
    Includes bibliographical references and index.
Identifiers: ISBN 9798986913001 (paperback) | ISBN 9798986913032 (Kindle) | ISBN 9798986913025 (eBook) | ISBN 9798986913049 (hardcover)
Subjects: LCSH: Work--Religious aspects--Christianity. | Work--Biblical teaching. | Employees--Religious life. | Vocation--Christianity.
Classification: LCC BV4593 .T75 2021 (print) | LCC BV4593 (ebook) | DDC 248.88--dc23

FAITH AND ENTERPRISE PRESS
Sierra Madre, CA 91025

Publisher's Note

This book is sold with the understanding that neither the publisher nor the author is providing psychological, financial, legal, or other professional advice. If professional advice or counseling is needed, the reader should seek help from a competent professional.

Table of Contents

Introduction

Many of us have a deep, intuitive desire to connect with something deeper than ourselves; while some might use different words, for many this means a deeper awareness of God and the divine mystery.

And we have a corresponding desire to allow this awareness, however we understand it, to inspire us as we live our lives and work with a renewed desire to make a positive contribution to the greater good and the well-being of other people.

We might not be aware of these desires for much of our lives, but from time to time they seem to emerge into our consciousness. And I believe that even when they remain hidden in our subconscious, they can still have a powerful effect.

When we are aware of these desires and express them through our work, it takes on new meaning—we might call this its sacred meaning. This involves who we are at the core of our being, how we relate to God and the great mystery, and how our work contributes to the well-being of others. It involves the biblical concept of shalom, or human flourishing, and how we deal with things that get in the way, especially sin, pervasive evil, and catastrophic misfortune. And it can involve spiritual practices that deepen our awareness of God as we work and follow our path of growth.

In a time of crisis, whether caused by economic difficulty or other factors, understanding the deeper meaning of our work can help us act with more courage and resilience. It can help us handle the challenges associated with being out of work when we are unemployed. And it can help us keep our spirit of enterprise and optimism as we overcome obstacles and seek new opportunities.

———

Our work is important, even apart from the income earned. It can significantly affect human flourishing, for both good and ill. On the negative side, it can be a source of stress, burnout, boredom, frustration, and interpersonal conflict. But work can also provide an opportunity to contribute to the greater good, pursue personal growth, develop and express a sense of purpose, and build friendships.

In this book, I hope to deal with both the positive and negative aspects of work in a way that you find helpful. Understanding its meaning and its spiritual dimension will, I believe, help us work with a new sense of purpose as we engage challenges and opportunities.

What would it mean to be more fully alive, purposeful, and compassionate as we work? To feel that we are contributing to the well-being of others? That we are dealing calmly with stress, burnout, and conflict? What would it mean for our faith or spirituality to inform and support our work in powerful new ways and remind us of our higher purpose?

The journey might not be easy. We sometimes face difficult challenges and connecting our spiritual journey with our work lives can, at times, be a struggle. Nevertheless, I believe it will be well worth the effort.

———

I think of the message of Jesus as an invitation to experience a deeper sense of connection with God and then express this through our work and other areas of our life. This might sound overly theoretical, but it has multiple aspects and the idea should become more concrete as we examine them.

The first aspect has to do with our mysterious relationship with God. There are many different ways to think about this and, in any case, the mystery of God is well beyond our comprehension. Yet most of us think of God as the origin of all that is, the ultimate truth, the source of life, and the incomprehensible yet personal power behind the world (or universe), driving it forward. Our faith or spirituality can provide ways to consider how we might participate in this divine movement.

The second aspect is our desire to contribute to the well-being of others and to society. This contribution might be the key to understanding how Jesus's instruction to "love your neighbor as yourself" can be translated into terms applicable to our work and business. This aspect is the basis for much of the meaning and satisfaction we find in our work, our working relationships, and the goods and services our work produces for others.

The biblical concept of shalom is the third aspect. We can think of shalom as a sort of holistic flourishing that starts with our relationship with God and with other people and extends into multiple dimensions involving all of human life, including spiritual, psychological, social, and economic well-being.

The concept of shalom can help us see the connection between the practical and spiritual aspects of our work. It can remind us that we are working toward a better world for ourselves and others.

Most of us seek personal transformation as we proceed on our spiritual journey; this is the fourth aspect. I usually refer to this transformation as spiritual and psychological growth and development. We want to become better people, escape from bondage to our surface egos, and be more like our true selves. This could mean some combination of being more loving, developing stronger character, handling misfortune with more composure, having a greater appreciation of life, and being more focused, effective, and wise as we work.

This transformation also involves sin and redemption, as well as the development of character strengths. Christian spirituality provides ways of confessing, repenting, and receiving forgiveness for sin, as well as for finding release from its burdens. It also aids in the development of virtue and character strengths.

These four aspects can help us better understand the spiritual significance of our work and how we might find a deeper sense of purpose, growth, and fulfillment as we engage in it. They can help us identify the ways that our work or business contributes to the greater good. And they can help us cultivate an enterprising spirit.

Reconnecting Spirituality and Our Work Lives

Throughout human history, people have had a desire for the sacred. We have had sacred times, sacred places, sacred objects, and sacred sounds. For as long as there have been human beings, the search for the sacred has been a natural and important part of what it means to be human.

This desire has at times been corrupted by other influences—tribal and cultural identity, attempts to use magic to influence spiritual forces, and the desire to justify religious or social authority.

But despite these corrupting influences, at the core of our desire for the sacred is a deep thirst for an experience of, or connection with, transcendent reality—with God—and the opportunity to carry this experience into the world and find meaning and inspiration for our daily lives.

Psychologist and scholar Kenneth Pargament of Bowling Green State University has spent several decades researching the psychology of religion and is known as one of the leaders in the field. He believes the search for the sacred is the essence of spirituality, the "core function of religion," and a "distinctive human motivation and process."[1] He has written:

> The most basic reason why people involve themselves
> in religion is because they yearn for something sacred
> in their lives. This is the fundamental motivating force
> behind virtually every religious tradition, and many
> (not all) religious institutions and individuals.[2]

For most of us, the sacred refers to God and the divine mystery. But it also extends beyond this sacred core to things and aspects of our lives that seem to express the sacred or that we associate with it in some way. As Pargament puts it:

> At the core of the sacred lie concepts of God, the
> divine, and transcendent reality. However, the sacred
> does not stop there; the domain of the sacred extends
> beyond to a ring that encircles the self, relationships,
> and place and time. In fact, virtually any aspect of
> existence can be seen through the sacred lens as a
> manifestation of God or as the container of sacred
> qualities.[3]

This suggests we might find sacred meaning in our work when, for example, it contributes to the greater good and the well-being of others. We might also experience it as we build relationships, integrate spiritual practices into our work lives, overcome sin and other obstacles, respond to a calling, and develop character and wisdom. Each of these can have a spiritual dimension and carry sacred meaning.

———————

There can be a tendency in some quarters to think of spirituality as applying exclusively to matters traditionally considered to be under the purview of the church. The language we use to discuss spirituality and the sacred can reinforce this tendency, making it more difficult to integrate our spirituality into the rest of our lives.

This tendency is unfortunate and can lead to a truncated and less potent faith or spirituality. Most of us interact with the world in significant ways through our work. Limiting our spirituality to only certain nonwork portions of our lives means that we will be less able to tap into the resources of our religious tradition as we interact with the world. We need a spirituality that informs our work and helps us find its meaning.

I have spoken with many devout Christians who are serious about their work but have trouble accepting the idea that their work has religious or spiritual significance beyond the need to treat people well and act with integrity. Most understand that their church teaches them to love their neighbors, including their coworkers, and be honest. When it comes to the goods and services their work provides, however, and the actual work dedicated to producing these, they do not see how their religion has any connection.

In my view, the main problem is not that people are not religious or spiritual enough, but rather that some theologies are too limited. Some people may have heard little or nothing in religious settings about how their work contributes to the greater good, except in those cases where someone makes a change in their work or business to do something that is more like charity (e.g., the contractor who does pro bono work to help build houses for the homeless).

I am convinced that we need a theology that offers a more holistic expression of the Christian faith, one that recognizes the contribution made by a broader range of jobs and people. Taking this approach would bring our theology more in line with what the Bible says about work.

––––––

By focusing on shalom and the greater good, staying grounded in prayer, and finding support in a theology that recognizes the contribution made by our work, I believe we can develop a positive and encouraging attitude that helps us through both good and bad times.

Societies and individuals have their economic ups and downs—some quite severe, as we have seen. But even in difficult times, we can look for opportunities, unmet needs, and new ways of connecting resources and talent. We can put together new initiatives that contribute to the rebuilding of the economy and the renewal of society and, in the process, create new jobs and business opportunities. And this applies even if we are not in a position to engage in something overtly entrepreneurial—we can still look for ways to make improvements within our own sphere of influence. With an enterprising spirit and a desire to help, we can be salt and light to the world.

This idea can be hard to accept when we are facing economic or personal stress, or when we are unemployed or in jobs that seem unsuitable for us. Nevertheless, it is important to keep striving to make things better. This might mean looking for new opportunities, but it can also mean staying where we are and doing the work in front of us as best we can, perhaps in new ways. In some cases, it might mean recognizing that our job might not have the intrinsic meaning we seek but that it can still provide the resources, even if only monetary, that allow us to move forward and express ourselves in the other parts of our lives.

––––––

We should note two caveats. First, religion, spirituality, and spiritual practices are important whether they help us in our work or not. The primary purpose of these is not to help us work more effectively or to become successful or wealthy, but rather to help us turn our attention toward God. But that does not mean that they cannot also help us in our work.

Second, while I am quite optimistic about the long-term future, some of us are going through hard times due to circumstances beyond our control. Some of us are unemployed or stuck in jobs or situations that feel oppressive and maybe even painful. Some of us face enormous time pressure, especially if we are working parents with young children at home, are working two jobs, or are taking care of elderly parents. Some of us have serious yet quite reasonable fears about the possible loss of our business or jobs. If this applies to you, I hope you find this book helpful as you look toward a better future.

The Challenge of Integration

This book is largely a work of integration. By this, I mean that it does not only apply a few standard theological propositions to the workplace without regard to the circumstances, but rather attempts to bring together information and insights from diverse sources. I believe that the Bible offers profound insights, but so do our own experiences at work. We can also draw heavily from contemporary research and from our understanding of businesses and other organizations. Real power comes when the insights and perspectives from different domains can be combined and allowed to work together.

It is also a work of integration in the sense that it connects ideas about the sacred with their application to various work-related issues.

As you read this book, your own spiritual experiences and perspectives will be especially important, particularly as they apply to your work. We each have spiritual intuitions, promptings, longings, and insights that can pull us in the right direction if we pay attention. That is why I refer to one's own faith or spirituality. It is your own faith or spirituality that is important as you read this book, not someone else's.

Even among those of us who consider ourselves Christian (and I would guess that most, but not all, readers of this book do), there can be considerable variation in how we see and experience our faith or spirituality and how this applies to our work. I hope you will reflect on the material presented from the perspective of your own faith or spirituality, whether you agree with my point of view or not.

The book will draw insights from the Bible and therefore a few words about the way scripture is being used would be in order. I would guess that many, and probably most, readers will have a more or less traditional understanding of scripture, but others will not and might even wonder why we are bothering with it. To the latter, I would suggest thinking of biblical scripture as the result of many thousands of years of humans grappling with the big issues such as who we are, how we relate to God, what is our purpose, what is the secret to human flourishing, and how are we to understand spiritual experiences and divine revelation. You might picture a great many successive generations sitting around fires at night telling the old stories, passing on insight and wisdom as their understanding developed. Insights about human work were an important part of these conversations.

The book will also incorporate material on Christian spiritual practices that you might find helpful. These will focus on prayer and related practices designed to help us become more aware of our deep spiritual promptings and intuitions and to become perhaps more open to listening for God in what I will call the sacred silence. I believe these practices can help us develop a deeper sense of mission over time, work with more purpose, energy, compassion, and wisdom, and deal with stress and other challenges calmly and effectively. Most of the practices will lend themselves to integration with your work life and were selected for this reason.

The major changes many of us face in our work lives can affect how we integrate our faith or spirituality and our work. These changes can include new communication practices (those associated with remote work, for example) that require us to find new ways to build community. We might also face an increase in personal agency (the ability and obligation to act on our own initiative) and rapid innovation in response to crisis and opportunity. I have added particular elements on the changing work environment where relevant, as well as a piece in the appendix that deals in more depth with these issues.

What To Expect From This Book

Understanding the sacred meaning of our work will help us understand its deeper purpose and how it contributes to the greater good. It will also help us understand and overcome obstacles and pursue opportunities.

Chapter One looks at human purpose and potential from the perspective of the two great biblical creation stories. The Bible suggests we have a deep, mysterious connection with God and expresses this in several ways:

we are made in the image of God, God breathed his spirit into us, and we were each created for a purpose. Each individual, therefore, has inherent value and dignity no matter their station in life.

We each have the right to act on our own volition and understanding, free from oppression. We are designed to enjoy creating and producing as we contribute to the greater good. These are essential aspects of our nature as humans and have profound implications for the meaning we find in our work.

Chapter Two explores the implications for human flourishing using the biblical concept of shalom as a starting point and then incorporates insights from contemporary resources, such as positive organizational psychology, to support and deepen our understanding.

Shalom originally meant flourishing in all dimensions of life, including (but not limited to) our work lives. As such, it provides ways to think about the meaning of our work and working relationships and how these connect with our faith or spirituality.

It takes many jobs and tasks for a modern society to flourish; shalom can help us appreciate these diverse and often unrecognized contributions.

Chapter Three discusses sin. As we talk about the potential goodness of work, many of us will recognize that our work lives do not reflect this high view, at least not on the surface. Sin is one of the things that spoil our work, corrupt our sense of purpose, and get in the way of shalom and flourishing. The chapter draws lessons from several examples and discusses the dynamics of confession, forgiveness, and reconciliation.

Chapter Four deals with other things that get in the way of flourishing and experiencing the deeper meaning of our work, such as adversity and misfortune. We discuss four that are especially important in our work lives: failure, work-related stress, burnout, and interpersonal conflict. The book seeks solutions from biblical insights, psychological research, and personal experience.

Chapter Five discusses cultivating character strengths that help us overcome sin and adversity, act with purpose, contribute to shalom, and develop productive, collaborative working relationships. It focuses on seven that are especially important in our work lives: integrity, courage, compassion, hope, humility, resilience, and prudence. Cultivating these strengths opens us to a life of spiritual depth and helps us work with greater purpose.

Chapter Six focuses on short spiritual practices involving various forms of prayer that can support and be integrated into the rhythms of our work. These practices help us turn our attention toward God as we go through the workday, develop a deeper sense of purpose and mission, stay calm in the face of crisis, and cultivate an enterprising spirit.

Chapter Seven explores whether our work can be our calling, with all this means for the purpose and fulfillment we find in it. The book explores the topic from secular and religious perspectives and offers suggestions for how we might develop a sense of calling over time.

Chapter Eight explores the spiritual dimension of leadership. It notes the difference between managers and leaders and the need both have for a clear sense of purpose. It discusses some of the temptations of leadership, such as narcissism, and includes a discussion of what the "shalomic organization" might look like.

The appendices include a more in-depth discussion of work in the Bible, a discussion of ongoing changes in the nature of work, an examination of the state of flow and whether or not it has a spiritual connection (a favorite topic of mine), and some thoughts about the opportunity for churches to meet the spiritual needs of people in the workplace.

Chapter One

Genesis: Human Purpose, Dignity, and Potential

What would it mean to work with a deeper sense of purpose? The Bible speaks to this and offers insights into our nature as humans, our mysterious relationship to God, our work's contribution to the greater good, and each individual's inherent dignity and potential.

The next two chapters offer for your consideration some of these biblical insights; these generally take a positive view of work and the connection between our work and our spirituality. Sin, of course, also enters the picture and spoils our work, as do various other problems; we will discuss these in later chapters, but for now our starting point will be to address the positive potential of human work. This is where the Bible begins.

The First Great Creation Story - Genesis 1

Many civilizations have creation stories that provide a foundation for how people see themselves. By going back to a supposed beginning, the creation story explains how the civilization originated and says something about the nature of the people and their culture; it is intended to place their lives into a meaningful context.

The Bible has two creation stories, both at the beginning. The first is Genesis 1, the first chapter of the first book in the Bible (it extends slightly past the end of Genesis 1 to Genesis 2:3). This story addresses the goodness of creation as initially intended by God. It describes how humans were made in the image of God with all this implies for the dignity and worth of the human person. This has important implications for our work life.

The origins of this first biblical creation story are somewhat murky. Whenever and by whomever it was written, the story was important to the Jews being held in captivity in Babylon, five to six hundred years before the birth of Jesus. For this reason, and to provide a sense of the story's importance and radical distinctiveness, it would be good to look at the Babylonian captivity as background.

Jerusalem, its Temple, and several other cities were conquered and completely destroyed by the Babylonian empire around 587 BCE (there were multiple invasions, over several years). Many Jews (perhaps twenty to twenty-five thousand) were taken into captivity in Babylon and were held there for more than fifty years, longer than a typical lifetime.

The Jews would have been exposed to their Babylonian overlords' own creation story, the Enuma Elish. This was a very different story than the creation story of Genesis 1. In the Babylonian story, there were many gods, and these gods eventually went to war against each other. A particularly cunning god by the name of Marduk led one of the factions. In a dramatic moment of the story, Marduk fought and killed the rival leader, Tiamat, who was also more or less the mother of the other gods.

After killing Tiamat, Marduk ripped her body in half and made the sky out of one half and formed the earth out of the other half. Later on, Marduk decided that the gods needed servants to do their work, so he killed one of Tiamat's defeated followers, cut him open, and used his bone and blood to form human beings as slaves who would serve the gods.[4]

Why was this story important? Perhaps partly because it showed order being brought out of chaos. But more importantly, the Babylonians were the chosen people of Marduk and therefore, according to the story, they had the power and authority to rule humanity on his behalf. And that is why the captive peoples were under the control of their Babylonian overlords and always would be. It sounds to me like this story was used as a tool of oppression.

Genesis 1 served as a counter to the Enuma Elish and other creation stories of the Ancient Near East. Unlike the Enuma Elish and the others, Genesis 1 has one all-powerful God, as opposed to a host of battling deities. And in the biblical story, God is good (as is his creation) and has created humans with value, dignity, and agency in their own right. He did not create humans to be slaves of the Babylonian oppressors.

I recommend reading Genesis 1:1-2:3. You might want to prepare by imagining what it would have been like to be one of the Jewish captives in Babylon. Imagine having to stand in a public square and listen to Marduk's story. Then imagine walking home in the late afternoon; the sun is still up, the dirt road is dusty and crowded. There is very little noise—maybe an occasional child or a quiet murmur, and the sound of feet.

As people return to their villages, they begin to gather in homes and meeting places—everyone, even the children. After everyone arrives, the adults close the windows, shut and latch the doors, and light a flame. And then they listen to a very different creation story, a story of hope, human dignity, freedom, and the possibility of flourishing lives.

> *In the beginning when God created the heavens and the earth, the earth was a formless void and darkness covered the face of the deep, while a wind from God swept over the face of the waters. Then God said, "Let there be light"; and there was light. And God saw that the light was good; and God separated the light from the darkness. God called the light Day, and the darkness he called Night. And there was evening and there was morning, the first day.*
>
> *And God said, "Let there be a dome in the midst of the waters, and let it separate the waters from the waters." So God made the dome and separated the waters that were under the dome from the waters that were above the dome. And it was so. God called the dome sky. And there was evening and there was morning, the second day.*
>
> *And God said, "Let the waters under the sky be gathered together into one place, and let the dry land appear." And it was so. God called the dry land Earth, and the waters that were gathered together he called Seas. And God saw that it was good. Then God said, "Let the earth put forth vegetation: plants yielding seed, and fruit trees of every kind on earth that bear fruit with the seed in it." And it was so. The earth brought forth*

vegetation: plants yielding seed of every kind, and trees of every kind bearing fruit with the seed in it. And God saw that it was good. And there was evening and there was morning, the third day.

And God said, "Let there be lights in the dome of the sky to separate the day from the night; and let them be for signs and for seasons and for days and years, and let them be lights in the dome of the sky to give light upon the earth." And it was so. God made the two great lights—the greater light to rule the day and the lesser light to rule the night—and the stars. God set them in the dome of the sky to give light upon the earth, to rule over the day and over the night, and to separate the light from the darkness. And God saw that it was good. And there was evening and there was morning, the fourth day.

And God said, "Let the waters bring forth swarms of living creatures, and let birds fly above the earth across the dome of the sky." So God created the great sea monsters and every living creature that moves, of every kind, with which the waters swarm, and every winged bird of every kind. And God saw that it was good. God blessed them, saying, "Be fruitful and multiply and fill the waters in the seas, and let birds multiply on the earth." And there was evening and there was morning, the fifth day.

And God said, "Let the earth bring forth living creatures of every kind: cattle and creeping things and wild animals of the earth of every kind." And it was so. God made the wild animals of the earth of every kind, and the cattle of every kind, and everything that creeps upon the ground of every kind. And God saw that it was good.

Then God said, "Let us make humankind in our image, according to our likeness; and let them have dominion over the fish of the sea, and over the birds of the air, and over the cattle, and over all the wild animals

*of the earth, and over every creeping thing that creeps
upon the earth."*

*So God created humankind in his image, in the image
of God he created them: male and female he created
them.*

*God blessed them, and God said to them, "Be fruitful
and multiply, and fill the earth and subdue it; and have
dominion over the fish of the sea and over the birds of
the air and over every living thing that moves upon the
earth." God said, "See, I have given you every plant-
yielding seed that is upon the face of all the earth, and
every tree with seed in its fruit; you shall have them for
food. And to every beast of the earth, and to every bird
of the air, and to everything that creeps on the earth,
everything that has the breath of life, I have given every
green plant for food." And it was so. God saw everything
that he had made, and indeed, it was very good. And
there was evening and there was morning, the sixth day.*

*Thus the heavens and the earth were finished, and all
their multitude. And on the seventh day God finished the
work that he had done, and he rested on the seventh day
from all the work that he had done. So God blessed the
seventh day and hallowed it, because on it God rested
from all the work that he had done in creation.*

Genesis 1:1-2:3[5]

Several aspects of the story might carry special meaning for us, starting with the idea that there is one God and this God is the source of all that is ("In the beginning when God created the heavens and the earth. . ."). There is no talk here of multiple gods or any divisibility or conflict among divine reality; God is the ground of being, to borrow theologian Paul Tillich's expression,[6] and the source of all of reality.

Unlike other creation stories of the time, including the Enuma Elish, this is not a story of supernatural beings misbehaving. It is an account of divine unity and purpose. God is the source and the creative force that is driving the world (the universe) forward.

God speaks all the elements of reality into existence. God intends something and it becomes real; his intention becomes concrete reality. Whatever God creates is good—very good, maybe by definition.

The images of the formless void, darkness covering the deep, a wind from God sweeping over the waters, and God speaking things into existence, are ways of grappling with the incomprehensible mystery of God and the ineffable quality of the infinite. But Genesis 1 also provides a link between divine reality and the concrete world in which we live. God speaks and the void is transformed; we can see, touch, and observe its material form.

And then, in verses 26 to 28, God creates humans in his image. There can be different views among theologians about what it means to be created in God's image, but it seems clear that in this story there is some sort of mysterious connection between God and humans and that we have been given a large degree of agency. By agency, I mean that we are able to act on our own volition and initiative and make decisions based on our own values and goals—or at least should be able to.

Verse 28 is sometimes called the creation mandate: on behalf of God, we are to produce and create, in other words, to work. The implication is that people have a deep, God-given drive to work with competence, effectiveness, and agency. This drive, I believe, is closely tied to our identity as humans. People should be allowed to bring their full talent to their work and thereby enjoy the status of co-creator.

Humans as Co-Creators?

Technically speaking, the Bible never uses the Hebrew word for "create" to describe human activity, only to describe God's activity. But this is more of a semantic issue than a real one. When the Bible speaks of God's creative action, it is speaking of creation *ex nihilo*, in other words, creating something out of nothing. In the Bible, only God can create something out of nothing; humans, on the other hand, take matter and energy that have already been created and convert them into something usable:

> *You [God] cause the grass to grow for the cattle,*
> *and plants for people to use*

to bring forth food from the earth,
and wine to gladden the human heart,
oil to make the face shine,
and bread to strengthen the human heart.
                                    Psalm 104:14-15

Looking at a modern example of the creative process, when the developers of the first iPhone invented their new product, they worked with matter that was already there, you might say converting preexisting atoms to new uses. But while this is not technically creating something out of nothing in the *ex nihilo* sense, we would nevertheless describe it as an act of extraordinary creativity and innovation (thank you, Apple developers!).

I would contend that if we look within ourselves, and think about our more positive motivations, we do, indeed, seem to be designed to create and build, improve our material circumstances, and constructively contribute to the greater good. It is inconceivable to me that our role is merely to maintain things as they are, without change. Most of us are more fully alive when we are creating, building, and innovating than when we are just maintaining the status quo.

Two Additional Perspectives

The second creation story begins at Genesis 2:4 and takes place in the Garden of Eden. It has an interesting perspective that relates to human agency and our spiritual connection:

> . . .*then the* LORD *God formed man from the dust of the*
> *ground and breathed into his nostrils the breath of life;*
> *and the man became a living being.*
>   Genesis 2:7

In other words, God formed the shape of the first human out of the dust, the lowest possible material, but the shape did not become a conscious human being until God breathed his spirit into him. This, too, suggests a deep connection with God.

The story then goes on to say that God placed the human in the Garden of Eden to "till it and keep it" (Genesis 2:15). In other words, in the Bible, work was part of our nature even before the expulsion from the garden; it is not the result of sin, though it might be spoiled by it.

The Bible also offers the idea that God designed and formed each of us individually before we were born, presumably for a purpose. For example, God tells the prophet Jeremiah:

> *Before I formed you in the womb I knew you,*
> *and before you were born I consecrated you;*
> *I appointed you a prophet to the nations.*
> *Jeremiah 1:5*

Lest we think this only applies to prophets and other famous persons, Psalm 139 speaks of humans more generally:

> *For it was you who formed my inward parts;*
>   *you knit me together in my mother's womb.*
> *I praise you, for I am fearfully and wonderfully made.*
> *Wonderful are your works;*
>   *that I know very well.*
> *My frame was not hidden from you,*
>   *when I was being made in secret,*
>   *intricately woven in the depths of the earth.*
> *Your eyes beheld my unformed substance.*
> *In your book were written*
>   *all the days that were formed for me,*
>   *when none of them as yet existed.*
> *Psalm 139:13-16*

We see somewhat similar examples of this perspective elsewhere, for example in Job 10:8-11, Isaiah 49:1, and Galatians 1:15. The point seems to be that God has formed each of us as distinct individuals with a purpose.

And so we are offered three complementary biblical ideas to help us think about our identity and purpose:

1. Genesis speaks of God making people in his image and placing his spirit within us.

2. It is in our nature to produce and create and thereby contribute to the greater good.

3. Each individual has inherent value, dignity, purpose, and the right to act on their own initiative.

What would it mean to more fully incorporate these ideas into our work? How would we do it?

Human Dignity

These biblical ideas speak to the dignity of each individual human. They suggest that each one of us has been created in the image of God and with God's spirit within us. No matter what our circumstances or station in life, we have a fundamental dignity and worth that should be respected. This applies to ourselves and to everyone with whom we come in contact.

Recognizing the fundamental dignity of our fellow humans, as unique individuals, has practical implications. We are more likely to form productive, collaborative working relationships with people whom we respect at a deep level. And people who are respected and valued as persons are more likely to bring their full talents and creativity to their work and to find purpose and pleasure in doing so.

People should also be free of coercion. Different individuals have different views of what the good life entails; recognizing their dignity means allowing them to pursue their own version of this, at least to the extent that it does not interfere with the rights of others.

Some employers see their employees as unique individuals and as valuable resources, while others seem to see them primarily as an expense. Seeing the potential in people and allowing them to develop and express it through their work (and elsewhere) can make a huge difference in their lives and the contribution they make to the organization's goals. Increasing numbers of employers have begun to see this.

I have seen this played out as I visited the plants of my company's suppliers. In some cases, it was obvious that people (I am thinking especially of line workers) were engaged in their work and seemed to feel that they were contributing. In one start-up in which I was involved, the production manager made sure everyone on the line knew they were responsible for the quality of the products and could reject items and even stop production on their own authority if they saw something that was not right. They were also encouraged to provide advice about possible process improvements as they gained experience. The people were respected as humans and took pride in their work and responsibility, and it showed.

On the other hand, I have seen plants with similar formal production processes but where the line workers were, for the most part, disengaged and just followed orders. Their productivity appeared to be quite different.

Dignity is not just a matter of kindness. I have seen situations where the owners or managers treated people very well and provided pay and other benefits well beyond the industry norm, but the employees nevertheless seemed bored and disengaged. I believe that, in at least some cases, this was because the work was designed in a way that removed initiative.

This illustrates the problem with seeing workers as people who need our compassion but not as individual agents capable of bringing talent and initiative to their work. People made in the image of God are capable of so much more than we sometimes realize.

At a church retreat several years ago, we watched a video about Max De Pree, who was the chief executive officer of the Herman Miller furniture company at the time. As De Pree interacted on the production floor with some of his line employees, it was evident that he encouraged people to bring their ideas and expertise into the discussion and to act on their own initiative. He recognized that they brought their unique talents to their work and had become the experts on their part of the manufacturing process.

Afterward, we broke into small groups for discussion. I asked my group (mostly small-business owners and independent contractors) to picture a conventional CEO who gives speeches about maximizing shareholder value, and to compare this image to that of Max De Pree as portrayed in the video.

20

Then I asked two questions:

> For whom would you prefer to work?

The response was immediate and unanimous: Max De Pree.

> Who do you think would be the most likely to
> maximize shareholder value?

Again, the response was unanimous (and enthusiastic): Max De Pree.

The reaction to the second question was especially interesting. I think it acknowledges what many of us know intuitively but do not often express— that people are more likely to be productive and engaged if they have a chance to apply more of their talents and insights to their work and to participate in creating and producing valued goods and services. Not all employees will respond positively to this opportunity, of course, but many will—and those who do so will drive the organization and determine its culture and values.

The Sacred Meaning of Everyday Work

Chapter Two

Shalom and Flourishing in the Workplace

The biblical concept of shalom, as originally understood, can help us develop a deeper, richer understanding of our work and its larger purpose. It can help us see the connection between spiritual and material aspects of our work and how both contribute to human flourishing. And it can provide a bridge to contemporary research into the components of flourishing work lives.

Shalom in the Bible

In the Bible, shalom involves completeness or wholeness and is meant to encompass all aspects of human life. It is grounded in our relationship with God and includes our relations with other people. From this starting point, it extends to peace of mind, prosperity, the end of hostilities, material well-being, good health, and life itself. Shalom is quite frequently associated with the Hebrew words for justice and righteousness, suggesting that these are included in shalom.

In contemporary terms, we might think of shalom as holistic, multidimensional flourishing that involves the spiritual, interpersonal, economic, relational, societal, psychological, and work-related aspects of our lives.

You might try imagining a workplace that fully reflects shalom and how multidimensional the effects would be. Our working relationships would be excellent. We would understand our contribution to human well-being, be purposefully engaged in our work, and experience fulfillment and satisfaction. I would also guess we could leave our work behind at the end of the day and enjoy our time away from the job, knowing that we had worked well. Shalom is certainly a worthy goal.

Shalom involves more than just a collection of positive elements. In the Bible, the components work together; a strong sense of connection with God means, in part, strong and compassionate social relations. These, in turn, encourage a robust, healthy society and a higher likelihood of overall economic prosperity. The integration of the various aspects is the key to understanding the power of the concept.

Shalom might involve an element of choice, at least to some extent; the Bible uses a dramatic story from the time of the early Israelites to make this point. Moses is dying as the Israelites are preparing to enter the promised land and establish a new society. He has spent several years laying out the various laws that have been given by God and preparing the people for this new challenge. Some of these laws deal with things like cleanliness and maintaining separation from other religions, but many other laws deal with commerce and with the ethics and social cohesion necessary to have a flourishing society.

Moses presents the people with a dramatic choice:

> *See, I have set before you today life and prosperity,*
> *death and adversity. If you obey the commandments of*
> *the* Lord *your God that I am commanding you today,*
> *by loving the* Lord *your God, walking in his ways, and*
> *observing his commandments, decrees, and ordinances,*
> *then you shall live and become numerous, and the* Lord
> *your God will bless you in the land that you are entering*
> *to possess. But if your heart turns away and you do not*
> *hear, but are led astray to bow down to other gods and*
> *serve them, I declare to you today that you shall perish;*
> *you shall not live long in the land that you are crossing*
> *the Jordan to enter and possess.*
> *Deuteronomy 30:15-18*

The people are given a choice: the way of shalom, leading to life and prosperity; or the way of sin, leading to death and adversity. We face the same decision today in our work; do we pursue shalom and hope to flourish? Or do we ignore it and face suffocating work relationships and purposelessness?

I do not believe that God will necessarily reward religious obedience with the fulfillment of our desires. But I do believe that individuals and societies tend to do better when they behave in healthy, life-giving ways.

This does not mean that people should be coerced to adopt a particular lifestyle or vocation. To say that people are more likely to flourish when they behave in particular ways does not mean that they should be forced into doing so, as long as they are not harming others. Shalom must also include respect for the dignity of the person and a recognition that the good life can mean different things to different people; this is part of what makes a free society interesting.

How might we move toward shalom? I think the two great commandments identified by Jesus address this and express the core of his ministry:

> *When the Pharisees heard that he had silenced the*
> *Sadducees, they gathered together, and one of them,*
> *a lawyer, asked him a question to test him. "Teacher,*
> *which commandment in the law is the greatest?" He*
> *said to him, "'You shall love the Lord your God with all*
> *your heart, and with all your soul, and with all your*
> *mind.' This is the greatest and first commandment. And*
> *a second is like it: 'You shall love your neighbor as*
> *yourself.' On these two commandments hang all the law*
> *and the prophets."*
>
> Matthew 22:34-40

When I consider the first commandment in connection with our work, I think of turning toward God in prayer and related spiritual practices that can help us connect with something deeper or bigger than ourselves. This is worth doing for its own sake but can also help us develop a deeper sense of purpose, act with more compassion, be open to stronger interpersonal relationships, and handle adversity with more patience (we will discuss prayer and other spiritual practices in more depth and specificity in Chapter Six).

As for the second commandment, I think of being more intentional about loving our neighbor, in this case, our coworkers, customers, and suppliers. This means treating people with compassion, understanding how our work serves others, and, in general, working for the greater good and the well-being of other people, including those whom our work supports.

These are the starting points of shalom in our work lives.

The Role of Material Well-Being

There can sometimes be a tendency in religious circles to overlook economics (especially market economics) and material well-being, except perhaps when it comes to alleviating the serious economic deprivation of the poor. This neglect can include not only attitudes toward money but also toward the goods and services our work provides to others. If a church does not recognize the value of the work people do, how can it minister to them in the workplace?

In the Bible, prosperity and the material well-being of the people are seen as worthy goals. This does not mean that we should idolize these or pursue them unethically. But if pursued with integrity and a proper sense of balance, the Bible treats them as worthwhile aspects of shalom.

In the earlier quotation, Moses includes prosperity of the people as a valued goal and there are many other examples to which we could look. The word shalom is sometimes used synonymously with prosperity:

> *May the mountains yield prosperity (shalom) for the*
> *people, and the hills, in righteousness.*
> > *Psalm 72:3*

> *O that you had paid attention to my commandments!*
> *Then your prosperity (shalom) would have been like a*
> *river, and your success like the waves of the sea.*
> > *Isaiah 48:18*

> *And this city shall be to me a name of joy, a praise and*
> *a glory before all the nations of the earth who shall hear*
> *of all the good that I do for them; they shall fear and*

> *tremble because of all the good and all the prosperity*
> *(shalom) I provide for it.*
>
> Jeremiah 33:9

Material well-being itself is valued in the Bible. This is implied in many places but is also frequently made quite explicit. God blessed Abraham with flocks, herds, silver, gold, camels, donkeys, and descendants (Genesis 24:35). Abraham's descendants will come out of Egypt with "great possessions" (Genesis 15:14). God will bless those who follow his rules with children, fruit, grape, wine, oil, cattle, flocks, land, good health, and security (Deuteronomy 7:12-15). Elsewhere, promised blessings include flowing streams, wheat, barley, fig trees, pomegranates, honey, iron, and copper (Deuteronomy 8:6-10; see also Leviticus 26:3-6, Deuteronomy 11:13-15, Deuteronomy 28:1-6, Joshua 24:13, Proverbs 10:22, and Isaiah 65:21).

And can anybody doubt that the goodness of creation described in the two creation stories (Genesis 1 and Genesis 2) had a material aspect?

These references can be a little embarrassing for people who, like me, oppose the notion of a prosperity gospel—the idea that God will reward obedience with wealth. I do not believe that God rewards obedience with material well-being, as though we were engaged in a transaction. But the Bible does see the material well-being of society as having value even if it is not guaranteed. Renunciation of material well-being has its place, but it would be wrong to see it as a primary theme of the Bible.

The Bible also sees industriousness as a positive value, as opposed to laziness:

> *The appetite of the lazy craves, and gets nothing, while*
> *the appetite of the diligent is richly supplied.*
>
> Proverbs 13:4

> *Let the favor of the LORD our God be upon us, and*
> *prosper for us the work of our hands—O prosper the*
> *work of our hands!*
>
> Psalm 90:17

There can, of course, be a dark side to work and commerce. The Bible often denounces work done dishonestly, without concern for others' well-being, or under coercion. We will speak more about sin later, but for now, let me say that I think we all know how sin can spoil our work—we have experienced this for ourselves. And prosperity must not be idolized (Proverbs 23:4–5); it is neither guaranteed nor permanent (see Job), nor can it be allowed to preempt our relationship with God and other people.

Our relationships with God and other humans are paramount, and we must not achieve wealth through crooked means. Healthy trade, markets, and collaboration add an important dimension to the satisfaction we get from our work, and these are easily spoiled by sin. Much of what we produce is developed in cooperation with other people, and trade magnifies these advantages as different resources and talents are brought to bear and exchanged. We undermine this if we behave in such a way as to damage our relationships and lose others' trust. This is true on all levels, from the individual to the corporate and governmental.

But let's not allow the presence of sin to make us forget that work is intended to be good and to be an essential part of shalom.

Shalom and Contemporary Work-Related Research

Over the last few decades, there has been an explosion of research into the psychology of work, motivation, positive psychology, and organizational behavior. Much of this research can be used to support and deepen our understanding of shalom in the workplace.

A flourishing society depends on high levels of personal productivity, as does the survival of our businesses. But shalom is also multidimensional. Not only does it involve the goods and services our work provides to others, but it is also reflected in our working relationships, the deeper meaning we experience in our work, and the feeling that we are contributing to the greater good. And, in accordance with the discussion in Chapter One, it recognizes each individual's inherent dignity, value, and agency.

Contemporary research suggests these values are usually complementary. For example, Harvard Business School Professors Teresa Amabile and Steven Kramer found in their research:

We discovered that people are more creative and
productive when they are deeply engaged in the work,
when they feel happy, and when they think highly of
their projects, coworkers, managers, and organizations.
But there's more. When people enjoy consistently
positive inner work lives, they are also more committed
to their work and more likely to work well with
colleagues.[7]

The conditions that support this form of well-being are not always
present. But when they are, the effect on shalom can be powerful.

In this chapter, we look at several of the contributions positive
psychology can make to our understanding of shalom (and vice versa).
Later chapters will refer to the work of other researchers who have made
contributions to our understanding of related subjects like hope, compassion, overcoming adversity, and finding meaning (see Chapters Four, Five,
and Seven).

Shalom and Positive Psychology

Researchers in positive psychology seek an evidence-based understanding
of the factors that lead to human flourishing and well-being. Martin
Seligman, a founder of the positive psychology movement, has identified
five elements (known collectively by the acronym PERMA) that provide a
framework. These include *positive emotions*, *engagement* (in other words,
absorption in what we are doing), *positive relationships*, *meaning* (this
can reflect our desires to contribute to the greater good and connect with
something larger than ourselves), and a feeling of *accomplishment*.[8]

Claremont University Professor Stewart Donaldson, Llewellyn
Ellardus van Zyl, and Scott Donaldson have suggested four additional
factors important for work-related well-being: *physical health*, *mindset*,
work environment, and *economic security*. They refer to the nine elements
together as PERMA+4.[9]

We can see how these nine elements represent important aspects of
shalom and contribute to flourishing in our work. Being engaged, having
good working relationships, and working with a positive attitude and a

sense of meaningfulness and accomplishment, contribute to shalom. And our work can, in turn, contribute to the economic security and health of ourselves and others.

In discussions of shalom, the Bible emphasizes our relationship with God, while with PERMA+4 the emphasis is different; it would not be appropriate or useful for social science research to make religious assumptions. Nevertheless, the overlap is extensive and we can see how positive psychology can make an important contribution to our understanding of shalom.

We can also see how our faith and spirituality can contribute to the elements identified by positive psychology researchers. Developing a sense of the sacred in our work certainly contributes to our overall sense of meaning. The teachings of our religious traditions encourage us to develop positive relationships. And our spiritual practices and the virtues taught by the church help us overcome sin, adversity and misfortune, develop a positive mindset, and live better lives. Each of these ideas will be developed further in future chapters.

Two other positive psychology research topics can make a contribution to our understanding of shalom at this point: Self-Determination Theory and the Dualistic Theory of Passion.

Self-Determination Theory

We have each probably observed that in some situations people can engage in tasks and other activities with curiosity, positive energy, a collaborative attitude, and creativity, but that in other situations the same activities evoke only boredom, disinterest, and disengagement. What makes the difference? And why does one set of circumstances seem to lead to personal growth and the other to stagnation?

Research psychologists and motivation experts Edward Deci and Richard Ryan have proposed, based on their research, that meeting three basic psychological needs encourages healthy functioning and growth in the workplace. These are the needs for competence, autonomy, and relatedness.[10] A sense of competence can be developed through successfully meeting challenges or performing tasks, from positive feedback, and from the sense that one is developing one's skills. Autonomy is the sense that one can act on one's own initiative and values (this does not mean that one is independent of other people). Relatedness means that we are known and appreciated, in this case by the people with whom we work.

Our social context can either encourage and support the fulfillment of these three basic needs, or it can suppress them. It can either contribute to our growth or limit it.

I believe this has clear implications for our work and our spirituality. At one level, community and healthy relationships are important for shalom, as are professional growth and the opportunity to act on one's own volition. At another level, when we are acting in accord with our internal drives and values, we are bound to be more authentic; our work is more likely to be an expression of our true selves and have spiritual meaning.

It is important to keep this in mind not only for ourselves but for the sake of our coworkers as well. As we work with people, whether in person or remotely, we should do what we can to allow them to express these needs in their work. Settings that foster positive relationships, encourage people to develop their skills (and be acknowledged accordingly), and allow them to act with a healthy degree of autonomy and initiative, will encourage more personal growth and productivity. They are also more consistent with the values expressed in Genesis 1 and elsewhere in the Bible.

The Role of Passion - Good and Bad

Canadian psychologist Robert Vallerand has focused his research on passion and observes that passion can lead to growth as we engage in activities with purpose and intensity. But not all passion is good, and not all passion leads to personal growth and flourishing.

Vallerand believes that there are two distinct types of passion: harmonious passion and obsessive passion. Harmonious passion is consistent with our internal drive for growth and is life-giving and energizing. With harmonious passion, we are in control; we can work hard, maybe even move into a state of flow, but when it is time to stop working and move on, we can leave the work and the particular passion behind and focus our attention on something else, such as our family. Harmonious passion does not override other aspects of our life and personality, and is more likely to lead to personal growth and well-being.[11]

Obsessive passion, on the other hand, has a compulsive quality. It can be difficult to leave the object of our passion, such as our work, behind when it comes time to stop. Because of the excessive importance we place on it, and the way it crowds out other aspects of our life and personality, we are more likely to be insecure and defensive about our work performance, and less likely to be open to new experiences and information. We are also more likely to spend time ruminating about what we may or may not have done well. Paradoxically, when we are working obsessively, it might also be more difficult to focus productively on the task at hand because we are distracted by our ego needs and external considerations such as how other people will evaluate the work we are doing.[12] We can expect that obsessive passion, instead of being energizing, can drain our energy and is more likely to lead to burnout.[13]

Does this mean that harmonious passion is always virtuous? While I would like to think so, this might be wishful thinking on my part. As with anything else, we should always endeavor to stay within moral and ethical guidelines, even when we are most passionate.

Vallerand does not write from a religious point of view. This is appropriate and perhaps even necessary as long as the discussion remains within a social science domain. But from a theological or spiritual point of view, we can see that there might be religious or spiritual implications to this line of thought. For one thing, harmonious passion contributes to shalom and obsessive passion works against it. Harmonious passion is more likely to enhance our relationships and engender feelings of peace and fulfillment in our work. And harmonious passion is more likely to lead to spiritual and psychological growth.

We might also speculate about a deeper spiritual connection. If we believe, as I do, that God is in some way working throughout all reality, driving it forward, and that he is accordingly working through our deepest drives and values and our deep desire to become the person that we are meant to be, then perhaps it is only a short step to the idea that when we are in a state of harmonious passion, we might be expressing not only our true selves but also something of God's Holy Spirit. There might be good reasons why the peace, fulfillment, and sense of purpose often associated with harmonious passion have also been traditionally seen as signs of spiritual growth.

This is not to say that either harmonious passion or meeting the needs identified by Deci and Ryan are necessary for spiritual growth. Sometimes working through difficult and even constraining times can be a source of growth as well. But it certainly appears that fulfilling these needs in our work will provide a better path for ourselves and our coworkers.

Our Work as Service to Others

Serving others and following Jesus's commandment to "love your neighbor as yourself" is central to Christian spirituality and our understanding of shalom. We are to serve other people and the well-being of society; much of our satisfaction in life and work is derived from our ability to do so.

But here we run into a problem—our understanding of how work serves others and the greater good can be much too narrow, especially when we consider it within a religious framework.

Several years ago, I launched a discussion program for small groups called *Transforming Work: Spiritual Renewal in Our Work Lives*; I designed it to help people see how their faith or spirituality might inform and support them in their work. I developed a curriculum for the program, farmed myself out as an itinerant small group leader, and took groups through a ten-week discussion program.

In the early sessions, I tried to focus part of the discussion on what the participants saw as the meaning and purpose of their work and its connection to their faith or spirituality. This, it seemed to me, was the appropriate place to start.

While there was a wide range of views, people frequently had difficulty connecting the purpose of their work with their faith or spirituality—even if their work was quite clearly beneficial to others. A couple of very devout participants even wondered if they should quit their jobs to do something that had more religious significance.

When discussing possible religious aspects of their work, people spoke of helping an employee in trouble, setting a proper moral example, or maybe even finding the right time to talk about their faith. But in these settings, they seldom discussed the value of the work itself and of the goods and services it provides to other people.

The auto repair mechanic did not say a word about the value of personal transportation. The caterer did not talk about how their work built shared memories and developed human relationships and community. And the lawyer and the accountant did not talk about how their work helped keep society organized and protected clients from the predatory behavior of others.

A participant in one of my discussion groups was involved with running a logistics department for a manufacturer and had a hard time seeing the value of his work from the perspective of his faith. Despite his difficulty making the connection, it was clear to me that were it not for jobs like his, we would all be growing our own food and making our own clothes—and spending most of our time doing so. The contribution people like him make to our well-being is enormous but he had trouble seeing its connection to his faith.

These discussions took place in religious environments or had a religious subtext and the participants understood that the purpose was to discuss their view of the connection between their faith and their work. Perhaps people would have an easier time talking about the purpose and value of their work in a more secular setting.

In more recent interviews, I have asked people to discuss their work in some depth before asking about their faith or spirituality. When talking about their work in isolation from these, they seem to more frequently describe the value of their work and the goods and services it produces.

But the perspective often changes when the conversation shifts to how their work is connected to their faith. While the responses are varied, many of these same people do not see how their work, and in particular the goods and services it produces, relates to their faith, aside from the need to treat people kindly and act with integrity. Their religious education apparently provides little affirmation for the work itself nor help in understanding its meaning and purpose.

I believe that many people are insufficiently aware of the contribution their work makes to the well-being of others and the greater good. And even among those who are aware of this contribution, many do not see how it connects with their religious tradition.

Why can it be so challenging to see the connections?

There seems to be a natural human tendency to separate the spiritual from the material and the sacred from the secular. Spiritual experience seems to contain hints of transcendence and the feeling that we are connected to something beyond the material world. And it is sometimes easier to experience this when we have mentally removed ourselves from our material circumstances.

But the problem goes beyond this natural inclination.

In some religious settings, the separation between the material and the spiritual is deliberately heightened, with the material devalued in favor of the spiritual. Sometimes asceticism is held up as particularly virtuous and material well-being is treated as an unworthy goal, except for helping those who face extreme deprivation. And at least a few theologians, pastors, and other religious leaders look askance at work in commercial enterprises, equating such commercial work with the caricatures of greed and narcissism presented by some of our commentators.

In my view, the problem is not that people are irreligious or leave their religion behind when they go to work, though this does sometimes happen. Perhaps they have not been in attendance when sermons affirmed the value of their work. But it might also be that their theology comes from a church or tradition that neglects the work life of its members or implicitly downplays their everyday work as compared to volunteer or other work the church sees as more congruent with its mission.

This is a serious problem. If we cannot see the religious or spiritual value in our work, then we not only cut ourselves off from the resources of our faith or spirituality in our work, but we also confine them to relatively small, restricted areas of our life. We are not living the full life promised by Jesus:

> *I came so that they may have life,*
> *and have it abundantly.*
>
> *John 10:10b*

———

In small group and other discussions, I have called attention to a passage from the book of Isaiah (61:1-4) as a starting point for reflection on the value of work, and I suggest reading it. Before doing so, however, it would be good to look at its background.

We previously discussed briefly the Babylonian captivity in the sixth-century BCE. The Babylonians were eventually defeated by the Persians and the Jews were allowed to return home, after fifty to sixty years of exile. They may have left Babylon with great excitement as they anticipated seeing their homeland, but when they arrived home they found their cities, including Jerusalem, in ruins and the Temple, which was the center of their civilization, destroyed.

As the people faced the daunting task of rebuilding the civilization, they heard these encouraging words from the prophet Isaiah:

> *The spirit of the Lord GOD is upon me,*
>> *because the LORD has anointed me;*
> *he has sent me to bring good news to the oppressed,*
>> *to bind up the brokenhearted,*
>> *to proclaim liberty to the captives,*
>>> *and release to the prisoners;*
> *to proclaim the year of the LORD's favor,*
>> *and the day of vengeance of our God;*
> *to comfort all who mourn;*
>> *to provide for those who mourn in Zion —*
> *to give them a garland instead of ashes,*
>> *the oil of gladness instead of mourning,*
> *the mantle of praise instead of a faint spirit.*
> *They will be called oaks of righteousness,*
>> *the planting of the LORD,*
>> *to display his glory.*
> *They shall build up the ancient ruins,*
>> *they shall raise up the former devastations;*
>> *they shall repair the ruined cities,*
> *the devastations of many generations.*
>>>> *Isaiah 61:1-4*

In this passage, our attention might naturally be drawn toward those aspects that represent overt acts of mercy, such as binding up the brokenhearted, comforting the mourning, and freeing the captives—and these are indeed essential. These are also the aspects of the passage that are most likely to be associated with religion and honored by churches.

But in the last lines the passage also addresses another aspect of restoration—rebuilding civilization. Here the prophet turns our attention toward restoring the material well-being of society.

Rebuilding a civilization, or even maintaining it, requires construction workers who will restore the walls and buildings. And by implication it also requires those who produce food and other goods, distributors and retailers, communicators, accountants and lawyers who keep chaos at bay, maintenance workers, administrators and advisors of a great many kinds, entrepreneurs, and many other occupations. A great many goods and services are needed to build and maintain a flourishing society; through our work, we serve other people and the greater good in many different ways.

While these varied occupations, and a great many others, all contribute to human well-being in ways consistent with the Christian faith, when we think in religious or spiritual terms, we often overlook their value.

This does not mean that we only work for the benefit of other people. Work provides the individual with other benefits, including income, the possibility of personal growth and development, and the building of community. Each of these benefits can be important in its own right, but knowing that our work also contributes to other people's well-being can be a source of additional satisfaction and fulfillment. It can also help us connect our work to our faith or spirituality.

Churches and preachers can play an important role by pointing out the value of our daily work, especially as it pertains to the goods and services our work provides. In addition to Isaiah 61:1-4, there are passages in Appendix A (Work in the Bible) that could be used as starting points.

Effective leaders of organizations often try to reinforce awareness of the contribution that each coworker is making to the greater good. This affirmation can be especially important for the people who serve in various support positions in which the contribution to customers might not be as clear as that of front-line coworkers.

Working individuals should not wait for affirmation, however. They themselves should reflect on how their work serves others and promotes shalom without waiting for institutional support.

It is crucial to get past the narrow confines that people often apply to this topic; as noted above, a flourishing society, characterized by shalom, requires a great many jobs and occupations. Caring for the sick, feeding the hungry, and looking after children and the elderly are all very important—but people contribute to the flourishing of society through their work in many other ways as well, and many of these do not fit the stereotypes of religious, spiritual, or charitable work.

Chapter Postscript

The Alleviation of Poverty in the Bible

While on the subject of shalom, we should say a few words about the Biblical approach to poverty alleviation.

Prosperity should generally help alleviate poverty by creating more opportunities and more material goods to go around. But beyond that, what else does the Bible say about alleviating poverty? I think three points summarize the general approach.

First, we should not take advantage of people who are on a lower economic rung. The Bible condemns taking their rights and property away in corrupt legal proceedings; people have a fundamental right to keep or trade what they have produced.

Second, we should give alms for people who are unable to support themselves and their families.

And third, people deserve the opportunity to work to support themselves. We see several policies in the Bible designed to promote this. For example, in the gleaning laws, fields were not to be harvested to the edge. Leaving a portion unharvested allowed poor and unemployed people to support themselves by harvesting the excess.[14] Note that the grain was not harvested for them, nor were they given free bread, but they were allowed into the field to work for themselves.

The anti-usury laws and the concept of Jubilee had a similar intent. In the agricultural society of the time, one bad crop year could wipe a family out and lead them into starvation. To avoid starving, they might be tempted to pledge their fields for a loan; that might provide the funds needed to feed themselves, but it also put them in jeopardy of losing the fields if they could not pay off their debt with the proceeds from the next crop season. They might also be forced to sell themselves or a family member into slavery. This threat of a bad crop was always present.

The solution for this risk of forfeiture was to forbid the making of loans that required the family's land as collateral or had interest rates that made the economic pressure on the family worse rather than better. And the Jubilee concept required that the land be returned to the original owners in specific years, thereby restoring their independence and their ability to work.[15]

The idea of human dignity is implicit in each of these biblical approaches. Relative to poverty, the lessons for our time are as follows:

- We need to maintain equal rights for the poor and the wealthy, especially under the judicial system, and not discriminate against the poor.
- We need to help people who cannot physically or mentally help themselves, and provide opportunity for people who are able to work.
- There is great value in building businesses that can employ or otherwise engage the talents of people. Even if the intent of a new business does not necessarily involve hiring the poor directly, increasing the number of jobs is bound to draw more people into the economy. Prosperous businesses, and new business formation, are critically important for providing people the opportunity to support themselves.

Along these lines, perhaps the key to reducing global poverty is to enable people to pursue opportunity and to help remove the obstacles that are in the way. If we think of global poverty as a billion or so mouths to be fed and bodies to be clothed and healed by outsiders, then it sounds pretty much unsolvable. If, on the other hand, we see it as a billion or so underutilized minds that can think and create and solve problems, then solutions might become possible as ways are found to liberate individuals and families from whatever constraints are holding them back. And this appears to be what has been happening over the last century as markets have expanded and become more open and obstacles have been surmounted. We can hope the trend continues.

Chapter Three

What Goes Wrong – Sin and Alienation

While work has the potential to be a place of shalom, it does not always live up to this high expectation. Many of us have not fully realized shalom in our work lives and do not usually feel that our work has spiritual significance. Something has gone wrong.

Multiple problems can interfere with our relationships, the sense of meaning and purpose we find in our work, and our ability to engage and be productive. Some of these involve sin; others do not but do involve forms of misfortune and adversity.

We are more vulnerable to these problems when we have lost our sense of purpose. And there can be a vicious cycle at work—as these problems pile up, they can distract us further from whatever sense of purpose we still have.

On a more positive note, however, there are things we can do to overcome these problems, move toward shalom, and renew the sense of meaning and purpose we find in our work.

This chapter will focus on sin, defining what we mean by the term and then using some examples to help us understand its nature. The last section of the chapter will deal with the challenge of reconciliation and the restoration of shalom. Then Chapter Four will deal with other types of problems involving misfortune and adversity.

The Problem of Sin

Quite often, the primary problem standing in the way of shalom is sin, whether our own or that of others.

We can define sin in various ways. Biblical scholars and theologians have referred to it as missing the mark, rebellion against God, and violating God's law. There is biblical warrant for each of these.

We can also think of sin as involving a condition of estrangement; the Bible generally thinks of this as estrangement from God, though often it implies estrangement from our fellow humans as well. Only equating it with estrangement, however, would neglect an essential aspect of sin—that of human culpability. By calling it sin, we add the guilt of culpability to the tragedy of estrangement.

Some biblical writers, such as Paul, seemed to see sin as an almost personal force that tempts us and draws us into evil. Sometimes the term refers to a power or condition, at other times to a particular act by an individual human. In any case, Paul and the others placed the responsibility for sin on human decision-making and moral failure, whether we are tempted by an outside force or not.

For our purposes, sin can be thought of as an act, a set of actions, or an attitude that is a moral or ethical violation and for which we are responsible. Specific sins include the so-called cardinal sins, such as greed, wrath, pride, lust, envy, gluttony, and sloth, and others such as dishonesty, cowardice, and a lack of compassion.

Sin works against shalom and the vision of holistic flourishing described in the previous chapter. In the workplace, it disrupts our work relationships, reduces our effectiveness, and spoils the satisfaction and pleasure we might otherwise experience. Most importantly, sin harms other people and works against the greater good.

Sin in the Workplace

In the Bible, the rules upon which early Israelite society was to be based included many designed to promote social cohesion. These included those we might consider the commercial laws of the time; violating these would certainly disrupt shalom. You might picture the disruption caused by someone stealing another person's property, courts making unfair judicial decisions in response to bribes, the use of false weights and measures, someone moving property lines when no one is looking, lying and violating contracts, unfair confiscations of property by government officials, and taking unfair advantage of people who are down on their luck. Each of these hurts people, disrupts shalom, and spoils our work and working relationships.

These sins were the focus of many of the early rules and also of the prophets who complained about what had gone wrong and issued warnings about the direction of society.

Our contemporary culture is radically different from that of the ancient Israelites, but we can still see how sin disrupts our relationships, violates our sense of fairness, and destroys the potential for shalom in our workplace and society as a whole. Today as then, any normal person feels some level of discomfort when they realize they have sinned against another person.

We can each identify the sins we think do the most damage to shalom in the workplace. My list would include dishonesty, a lack of concern for others, narcissism, and indolence. We can also include resentment, an inclination to gossip, and envy. Even apparently minor sins like these can block shalom in the workplace by disrupting our relationships and poisoning our attitude.

There are also sins that combine perverse economic incentives with dishonesty and represent a form of petty theft. The prevalence of these depends on the culture and the level of temptation, but in any case, there are reasons why invoices and shipping documents need to be checked, cash and inventories monitored, and expenses audited.

The Story of Cain

The story of Cain is a particularly vivid example of sin in the workplace and its damaging consequences. It has much to say about the dynamics of sin and why sin can do so much damage, even to the point of creating a toxic workplace. While we are unlikely to experience anything this bad in our own work lives, the extreme nature of Cain's sin and alienation can help us see the dynamics more clearly—dynamics that also apply to smaller, less dramatic sins.

Cain and Abel were brothers, but they were also coworkers of sorts. They appear to have had different jobs and skills—Abel looked after the sheep and Cain was a farmer—but both contributed to the family enterprise.

> *Now the man knew his wife Eve, and she conceived and bore Cain, saying, "I have produced a man with the help of the LORD." Next she bore his brother Abel. Now Abel was a keeper of sheep, and Cain a tiller of the ground.*
>
> *In the course of time Cain brought to the LORD an offering of the fruit of the ground, and Abel for his part brought of the firstlings of his flock, their fat portions.*
>
> *And the LORD had regard for Abel and his offering, but for Cain and his offering he had no regard. So Cain was very angry, and his countenance fell.*
>
> *The LORD said to Cain, "Why are you angry, and why has your countenance fallen? If you do well, will you not be accepted? And if you do not do well, sin is lurking at the door; its desire is for you, but you must master it."*
>
> *Cain said to his brother Abel, "Let us go out to the field." And when they were in the field, Cain rose up against his brother Abel, and killed him.*
>
> *Then the LORD said to Cain, "Where is your brother Abel?" Cain said, "I do not know; am I my brother's keeper?" And the LORD said, "What have you done? Listen; your brother's blood is crying out to me from the ground! And now you are cursed from the ground, which has opened its mouth to receive your brother's blood from your hand. When you till the ground, it will no longer yield to you its strength; you will be a fugitive and a wanderer on the earth."*
>
> *Cain said to the LORD, "My punishment is greater than I can bear! Today you have driven me away from the soil, and I shall be hidden from your face; I shall be a fugitive and a wanderer on the earth, and anyone who meets me may kill me."*

Then the LORD said to him, "Not so! Whoever kills
Cain will suffer a sevenfold vengeance." And the LORD
put a mark on Cain, so that no one who came upon him
would kill him. Then Cain went away from the presence
of the LORD, and settled in the land of Nod, east of Eden.
Genesis 4:1-16

In this story, God seems to favor Cain's younger brother, Abel, for unknown reasons, and so Cain is naturally resentful. God advised him to get his anger and resentment under control, but Cain ignored the advice and allowed his negative emotions to dominate him. He then murdered his brother.

The story is a dramatic example of how sin can lead to estrangement and alienation. As a result of his brother's murder, Cain became alienated from society, from creation, and from God. Murder is a particularly grievous sin and therefore can make the dynamics of sin especially clear. Nevertheless, even small sins like petty resentments and envy can lead us into a degree of alienation.

Each of us can point to particular sins we have seen in the workplace and how they disrupted shalom. But before we judge others too harshly, we should recognize that we each sin and that consequently we each bring at least some sin into the workplace. Knowing this, and taking steps to minimize the harmful effect of sin on our relationships, can take us a long way toward redeeming our work lives and developing a healthier working environment.

Becoming aware of our own sin is probably the best starting point; self-reflection and self-awareness can go a long way toward minimizing its harm. It might also teach us to act with a higher degree of forbearance and patience with others as they, too, bring sin into the workplace.

A Story of Greed and Excessive Self-Concern

The story of King Ahab, Jezebel, and Naboth presents another example of sin. To summarize it:

King Ahab desired the garden (a farm, most likely) of
Naboth, who was one of his subjects, but Naboth refused

to sell it to Ahab because it had been in his family for many generations and had special significance for him.

Ahab was unhappy about not being able to have the farm. Therefore, Jezebel, the king's wife, plotted to steal it from Naboth. She arranged for a meal in Naboth's honor and then for two ne'er-do-wells to bring false charges against Naboth at the event. The ruling elders of the town were in on the plot and had been instructed by Jezebel to pronounce Naboth guilty and then to stone him to death. They then did so.

Upon receiving the news of Naboth's murder, Ahab took possession of the innocent man's land, pretending that nothing was amiss and that proper procedures had been followed.

Adapted from 1 Kings 21:1-16

In this story, a leader with great power succumbs to temptation and is utterly insensitive to the rights and feelings of a less powerful person. Ahab appears to be oblivious to the great evil and pain he is inflicting; he had been blinded by temptation and perhaps a sense of entitlement.

I doubt that any readers of this book will murder innocent people to steal their land. But I think the story teaches about the risk of succumbing to temptation and inflicting harm while being insensitive to the consequences. This can apply to much smaller issues in the contemporary workplace.

I believe that most people with whom we are likely to work try to be honest and do the right thing. But we can nevertheless be tempted in ways that seem relatively minor; an example might be something like withholding information from a coworker to get a leg up on a promotion. Or perhaps it might be overlooking a supplier's error that results in an under-billing.

These might not be big issues, and we each probably succumb occasionally to minor temptations. But while the magnitude might be small, minor sins nevertheless undercut our relations by betraying trust and goodwill. And most of us who have been in business for a while have learned this lesson, often the hard way: we need to be trustworthy in small things if we are to be trusted in large ones.

Temptation and the Downward Cycle

King David provides another example of sin. David was regarded as a great king by the Israelites and a favorite of God. Nevertheless, he was also capable of great sin.

One day, David saw the beautiful Bathsheba, wife of the loyal soldier Uriah, bathing on the roof of a building below him. He was possessed by lust, so he had Bathsheba brought to him and had sex with her.

Bathsheba became pregnant. David arranged for Uriah, who was off fighting in one of David's wars, to be brought home to his wife in an attempt to make it look like the baby was from Uriah. But Uriah refused to sleep with Bathsheba while his comrades were in danger at the front. Therefore, David hatched a new plan: he had Uriah sent back to the front and placed in a position of extreme danger. The brave and honorable Uriah was killed.

David waited a suitable period of mourning and then married Bathsheba, behaving as though nothing was wrong. But the prophet Nathan thought otherwise and confronted David. By the end of the exchange, the reader can feel the weight of David's guilt:

> *But the thing that David had done displeased the*
> *LORD, and the LORD sent Nathan to David. He came to*
> *him, and said to him, "There were two men in a certain*
> *city, the one rich and the other poor. The rich man had*
> *very many flocks and herds; but the poor man had*
> *nothing but one little ewe lamb, which he had bought.*
> *He brought it up, and it grew up with him and with his*
> *children; it used to eat of his meager fare, and drink from*
> *his cup, and lie in his bosom, and it was like a daughter*
> *to him.*
>
> *"Now there came a traveler to the rich man, and he*
> *was loath to take one of his own flock or herd to prepare*
> *for the wayfarer who had come to him, but he took the*

> *poor man's lamb, and prepared that for the guest who had come to him."*
>
> *Then David's anger was greatly kindled against the man. He said to Nathan, "As the* Lord *lives, the man who has done this deserves to die; he shall restore the lamb fourfold, because he did this thing, and because he had no pity."*
>
> *Nathan said to David, "You are the man!"*
>
> *2 Samuel 11:27b - 12:7a*

Here again, we see the danger of succumbing to temptation. And we can also see how the sin can seem to multiply if we do not get off the wrong track quickly; the longer we try to hide from the results, the worse they get. In David's case, lust proceeded to adultery, then to deceit and trickery, and then to the murder of a virtuous, loyal man. It would have been tough for David to confess to the sin of adultery when Uriah returned home, but covering it up by scheming for Uriah's death made it so much more evil.

The application to the workplace is obvious. Of course, we need to resist temptation. But maybe even more important, when we do wrong, we must not let the progression of cover-ups and excuses continue. The cover-ups make it much worse.

———

These are dramatic examples. But we also need to be alert to the small temptations and small cover-ups that are more common in our work lives. A transgression that starts small can quickly build into something more significant as we progress through the cover-up stages. And this can be very damaging to our relationships and to shalom.

Disconnection from Reality

Our emotions can drive us to sin. Cain was resentful after his pride was hurt; Ahab was motivated by greed; and David was driven first by lust and then by the fear of his sin being discovered. We can hope that our motives are more virtuous and should certainly try to work in this direction. But even if sinful motives remain, we must not act on them; as God said to

Cain, "sin is lurking at the door; its desire is for you, but you must master it."

Sin has a way of disconnecting us from reality—we can be so dominated by an emotion that we lose touch with the consequences of our action and the harm we inflict on others. You might say we become desensitized, at least temporarily. I think that for many sins, if we just stopped and considered the harm we were about to do, we would not do them. There might be sociopaths who cannot feel someone else's pain and might actually enjoy inflicting it. But most of us are not like that. If we take the time to know the people that our actions affect, most of us would behave differently. And even if we do not know the people affected, we can still take the time to try to understand how our actions might harm them.

Sometimes part of the problem is cowardice. In the case of Ahab and Naboth, the town elders agreed to have Naboth stoned on false pretenses. I would guess that they went along with it out of fear; in some cases, we need stronger character to resist temptations and act courageously.

———

There can seem to be a petty, small-minded quality to sin. It is not that the damage it does is small—in all three examples in this chapter, the results of sin included the death of an innocent person. Nor is it that the temptations are small; in our examples, David had strong reasons to resist exposure, and both Cain and Ahab were overwhelmed by the power of their emotions, anger and hatred in one case and greed in the other.

It is from the perspective of shalom and our deeper purpose that sin seems small-minded. When confronted with Moses's choice between life and prosperity, or death and adversity, we choose sin and death. Rather than choose shalom and all that might mean, when we sin we usually choose something much smaller and more transient.

In our work lives, our sins can be quite small but still disrupt shalom. When we hurt someone, it is sometimes inadvertent; we make a mistake that hurts someone else. But sometimes it is indeed our fault, for example, when we speak up too quickly or carelessly and our hidden resentment or pride momentarily slips out and damages the other person. Or we engage in a bit of dishonesty to gain an advantage. Sometimes we are the perpetrator, and sometimes we are on the receiving end. Most of us have probably been on both sides, and more often than we care to admit.

Restoring Shalom After Sin

Despite its apparent pervasiveness, sin is not the end of the story. There are things we can do.

Part of the answer can be found in Chapter Five, on developing character strengths, and Chapter Six, on spiritual practices that can be integrated into our work lives. I believe developing our character and engaging in spiritual practices such as prayer can help us reduce our propensity to sin. And Chapter Eight, on spiritual aspects of leadership, addresses the risk of narcissism in leaders.

But despite our best efforts, we still sin, even if not as much as might otherwise be the case. How can we then reconcile with others and begin to restore shalom after they or we have sinned against the other person?

Most versions of Christian doctrine point to the forgiveness of sin by God, with the idea that God promotes reconciliation and welcomes us back, not holding our sins against us. In the words of the Apostle Paul:

> *So if anyone is in Christ, there is a new creation:*
> *everything old has passed away; see, everything has*
> *become new! All this is from God, who reconciled us to*
> *himself through Christ, and has given us the ministry of*
> *reconciliation; that is, in Christ God was reconciling the*
> *world to himself, not counting their trespasses against*
> *them, and entrusting the message of reconciliation to us.*
> *2 Corinthians 5:17-19*

But what about our relationships with other people, and especially our coworkers? How do we repair our relations with them? I know that in my own case, it is in my relations with other people that I am likely to feel the effects of my sin most acutely. And I suspect I am not alone in this.

Each of us is both a sinner and a victim of sin, though perhaps at different times, and so we should be concerned with both sides of the reconciliation process. The New Testament calls on us to confess and repent of our sins and to forgive people who sin against us. Beyond this, it offers several somewhat different perspectives. We are to forgive others because God has, or will, forgive us (Matthew 18:22-35, Mark 11:25). We are to forgive people if they confess and repent; in some cases, this might mean confronting them first (Luke 17:3-4). But the overarching view seems to be that we are to love and forgive people whether they confess and repent or not; this seems to me to be the most important point. Jesus expressed this most dramatically as he was painfully dying on the cross:

> *When they came to the place that is called The Skull,*
> *they crucified Jesus there with the criminals, one on his*
> *right and one on his left. Then Jesus said, "Father, forgive*
> *them; for they do not know what they are doing."*
>
> Luke 23:33-34

Situations and people vary greatly. We each have to decide for ourselves how best to bring about reconciliation within the circumstances we face. The goal remains the restoration of shalom, but how we get there is not always clear.

In *most* cases, the quality of the relationship can be a determinant of how likely reconciliation will be. Relationships that have been conducive to an open exchange of views and concerns, are based on a mutual concern for each other's well-being, and recognize the fundamental human dignity of each person are likely to be more amenable to reconciliation when things go wrong. Both parties will be more likely to extend grace to each other.

I suppose there might conceivably be cases when other factors come into play that argue for withholding an expression of forgiveness. And some offenses might be so serious, and so detrimental to the workplace and to other people, that something more might be required.

But in most cases, we need to get to the point where forgiveness takes place. If we cannot forgive someone, then we are probably not going to be able to reestablish a strong working relationship either. The same applies to repentance; if we are not willing to repent and apologize for harm we have done, then here, too, reestablishing the relationship will be difficult.

On the other hand, if we can forgive, or conversely, if we can apologize and repent, there is usually a good chance that we will be able to renew our relationship and get back on the path to shalom. We might even find that the relationship becomes stronger than it was before the harm occurred. Maybe we will even experience a bit of joy as reconciliation takes place.

Chapter Four

What Goes Wrong – Misfortune and Adversity

Sin is not the only thing that can disrupt shalom, spoil our work, and keep us from experiencing its deeper meaning. We are also subject to problems that may not be our fault, at least not in a morally culpable sense, but still represent forms of misfortune or adversity.

These problems can be the result of external factors, including economic downturns (or worse), pandemics, international conflict, market change, industry restructurings, or just plain bad luck. Each of these can cause serious harm for a great many people.

There are also forms of adversity that affect us individually. This chapter will focus on four that are of particular importance in our work life and that usually require a response from us: 1) failure; 2) stress; 3) work-related burnout; and 4) interpersonal conflict. Each of these has both practical and spiritual dimensions.

I discuss these four issues separately from sin because sin is not necessarily involved. Of course, sin *might* be involved; envy, pride, and excessive self-concern can certainly contribute to stress, interpersonal conflict, and, especially in the case of corruption, failure.

While misfortune and adversity do not necessarily represent a moral failure, they often involve spiritual and personal estrangement, either as cause or effect. We can see this in the stories included in this chapter. Peter becomes separated from Jesus and loses his courage before regaining it later, apparently through a spiritual experience. Elijah is completely burned out and has given up on life and his work until he encounters God in the sheer silence of the cave.

———

Before proceeding, I would like to point out two things about what follows.

First, things like failure, stress, burnout, and interpersonal conflict can be painful to experience and even to discuss. But I think that understanding them better can help us deal with them more effectively and perhaps move toward shalom.

Second, I believe it is important to examine these problems from both spiritual and so-called secular perspectives, and I try to do so. As I express my opinions, however, please note that I am not a trained professional in psychology, The reader should look to someone else if they believe that professional help might be useful in their situation.

Failure and Setbacks

I think most of us have gone through times when we seemed to be going backward in our career or work life. We may have been in situations where we have failed and seemed dead in the water while everyone else was moving forward. Or maybe we lost our job and found ourselves unemployed and worried about our family's economic survival. Maybe you are going through something like this now, but whether you are or not, I think you probably know what I am talking about.

When we have failed, we cannot go back and change the decisions and events that led to this happening. But we can at least determine our response to our failure, and it is our response that will usually be the most important factor over the long-term. There are no guarantees, of course, but there are plenty of examples of people who have failed and eventually bounced back stronger.

While we might feel like we are moving backward in these situations, I wonder if this is necessarily true at a deeper level. Perhaps something is going on out of sight, something that is laying the foundation for new growth, something of which we might not be aware. It is not unusual for people, as they get older, to look back on those times when they thought they were stuck and realize that these periods were essential for their subsequent growth.

Here is a story from my own work life. Thirty plus years ago, I had a good job at one of the largest consumer product companies in the world.

I had successfully started a new business for them and things were going well. Nevertheless, I allowed myself to be recruited into a smaller company that was going through a leveraged buyout. As you might be guessing, the company I joined failed miserably. It was in trouble maybe a month or two after I joined and failed completely a few months later.

I did not have an income, so I started distributing sandwiches, burritos, and pastries to convenience and liquor stores. I think I was making much less than the minimum wage, when I made anything at all. It was fortunate that my wife was working.

Things eventually worked out, as they usually do; I managed to identify a much better opportunity. And then, with the help of a few very good people, some good luck, and a lot of hard work, we managed to build a business that has worked out quite well over the years. I recently sold the business after building it for thirty years.

There is hope. We might not be able to change our objective circumstances, at least in the short run, but as I said, we can control our response to these circumstances. In my case, my response was far from perfect. But eventually (partly because of economic need), I was able to start thinking in terms of opportunity and growth, rather than failure and negativity, and found a way forward.

I would like to say that my religious faith helped me get through the crisis, but the fact is that I had no interest in religion or spirituality at the time. That came later. But I am convinced that I would have handled the situation better, and been more effective on the rebound, had I had a deeper religious or spiritual life. Prayer would have helped.

There are things we can do when we are facing these situations. We can endeavor to remain optimistic. We can build our resilience by accessing our social support networks and engaging in exercise and other leisure-time pursuits. We can make this a time of learning and development and of exploring new opportunities for growth. We can explore new interests and possibilities.

Aside from prayer, I think the most important thing is to maintain and maybe even strengthen our sense of personal agency. Rather than seeing ourselves as passive victims, we need to maintain the sense that we have the power to decide how we are going to respond to the situation. We might not be able to change it, at least in the short run. But we can continue to look for ways to change it in the long run.

And we can continue to learn and develop our abilities. We can also pursue excellence in whatever we are doing, even though it might not seem very important at the time. Establishing or building the habit of excellence can be an important strength for the future. This can make it more likely that we will break through the oppressive circumstances sooner rather than later.

There is something about continuing to do excellent work, no matter what the situation is, that seems to make it more likely that opportunities will come our way. This can also help us be more alert to the possibilities. And, meanwhile, we can continue to maintain and strengthen our spiritual values and aspirations. By doing so, we might find the meaning and purpose that cannot be provided by cold circumstance.

Most important, we can pray and seek spiritual strength. We can respond to difficult times in ways that enhance and fortify our spiritual journey and our spiritual life. And these can be an important source of strength. No matter what our circumstances, whether we seem to be moving forward or backward in our career, experiencing success or failure, or are employed or involuntarily unemployed, we nevertheless have an opportunity to turn our attention toward God in prayer and other spiritual practices and to strengthen our sense of connection and our spiritual character. And if we develop the ability to turn our attention toward God in the face of these distracting troubles, the resulting character development is likely to be more profound.

This does not mean it is easy. I do not know about you, but I certainly do not find it easier to pray during times of stress, though it is still quite possible to do so if that is our intention. And when a crisis comes, it is hard to be at peace and to bring to the foreground a natural sense of composure. But this, too, is possible.

––––––––

The actions of the Apostle Peter on the night of Jesus's arrest provide an especially dramatic example of failure and eventual redemption. When Peter learned that Jesus would be arrested, he bravely pledged that he would follow and defend Jesus, even to the point of his own death; he clearly saw himself in heroic terms. But when, during the trial of Jesus, servant girls and other bystanders accused Peter of being a follower of Jesus, he denied it three times.

Here is how Matthew tells the story:

> *When they had sung the hymn, they went out to the Mount of Olives.*
> *Then Jesus said to them, "You will all become deserters because of me this night; for it is written, 'I will strike the shepherd, and the sheep of the flock will be scattered.' But after I am raised up, I will go ahead of you to Galilee."*
> *Peter said to him, "Though all become deserters because of you, I will never desert you." Jesus said to him, "Truly I tell you, this very night, before the cock crows, you will deny me three times."*
> *Peter said to him, "Even though I must die with you, I will not deny you." And so said all the disciples.*

Later, after the arrest of Jesus:

> *Now Peter was sitting outside in the courtyard. A servant-girl came to him and said, "You also were with Jesus the Galilean." But he denied it before all of them, saying, "I do not know what you are talking about." When he went out to the porch, another servant-girl saw him, and she said to the bystanders, "This man was with Jesus of Nazareth." Again he denied it with an oath, "I do not know the man."*
> *After a little while the bystanders came up and said to Peter, "Certainly you are also one of them, for your accent betrays you." Then he began to curse, and he swore an oath, "I do not know the man!"*
> *At that moment the cock crowed. Then Peter remembered what Jesus had said: "Before the cock crows,*

you will deny me three times." And he went out and wept bitterly.

Matthew 26:30-35, 69-75

Failure can be caused by factors outside of our control. Or it can be caused by our own mistakes and misjudgments. In Peter's case, it may have been cowardice that caused his failure to live up to his expectations.

But within days, something changed. Despite his failure on the night of Jesus's arrest, Peter went on to become the powerful leader of the new movement and eventually faced martyrdom in Rome.

Both Luke and Paul wrote that, after his death, Jesus appeared first to Peter, before the other disciples (Luke 24:34, 1 Corinthians 15:5). Neither writer describes this experience, but we can see the profound result: Peter the bumbling failure became Peter the strong, visionary leader.

Peter's spiritual experience changed him and gave him courage and a new sense of mission. As a result, it was not Peter's failure that mattered most, but his response. Perhaps this, too, suggests the value of turning our attention toward God in prayer when we are facing failure.

Work-Related Stress

Stress is a big problem in many of our work lives and is a severe disruptor of shalom. It is usually difficult to see the deeper meaning of our work when we are preoccupied with stress or anxiety.

Almost all of us experience stress from time to time and know how it negatively affects our sense of well-being, our health, and our work. Our worries create painful emotions that demand our attention. They can make it more difficult to think clearly; we might become less rational when stressed. And our worries can isolate us from other people.

But there are things we might do to help reduce its harmful effects on ourselves and others, especially if we can better understand its causes.

––––––––

The way we see the world and our situation can be crucial. Psychologist Richard Lazarus did important work in this area, adopting what he described as a transactional approach to stress and related emotions. He saw stress as originating in an unsatisfactory relationship between the environment and the individual, as appraised or evaluated by the individual.[16]

This last element, the way the individual appraises the situation, is critical. It is part of why different individuals respond to situations differently, and why the same individual can respond to essentially the same situation in different ways, depending on where he or she is in their life.

One especially important aspect of this appraisal process is whether or not we believe we have the resources (tangible and intangible, material, psychological, and spiritual) necessary to deal with the situation. If we do not believe we have the resources, our stress level is likely to go up. On the other hand, if we do believe we have the resources, then we are more likely to deal with the situation as a manageable challenge.[17] This confidence can make all the difference and has obvious religious and spiritual implications.

As the Apostle Paul said:

> . . . *for God did not give us a spirit of cowardice, but*
> *rather a spirit of power and of love and of self-discipline.*
> *2 Timothy 1:7*

Unhealthy Rumination

When we cannot shake off our worries, we might find ourselves in a counterproductive rumination cycle that blocks us from experiencing shalom and the activities and relationships we find enjoyable. It might be difficult for us to think about anything else, even after leaving work. We can become dominated by our regrets over past events and our worry about future things that could go wrong. This works against shalom and our ability to attend to our human and spiritual relationships; even something like prayer can be disrupted as our attention is forced back to our worries.

Stress and this rumination cycle can also diminish our effectiveness at work and make it more difficult to find purpose and fulfillment. Sometimes the worry is necessary and productive; there are difficult things to which we need to attend. But this is different from the unproductive and painful rumination that does us no good and burns up so much of our time and energy.

Clinical psychologist (and friend of the Center for Faith and Enterprise) Scott Symington has done considerable work in this area, developing ways to bring the principles of mindfulness to bear on our worries.[18]

Symington recognizes that to end the painful, counterproductive rumination cycle, we need to get control of our attention and tether it to the present moment, focusing on the here and now and on the things we find to be life-giving, including our spirituality. While there are times when we need to address our fears and worries, we cannot become enslaved to them nor allow them to dominate our attention when it is not productive to do so. We can acknowledge and make space for these worries, but then we need to redirect our attention to the present moment and other life-giving aspects of our life.

In his book *Freedom from Anxious Thoughts & Feelings: A Two-Step Mindfulness Approach for Moving Beyond Fear and Worry*, Symington proposes an imaginative tool to help us do this. He suggests we imagine our internal world as having two screens—the Front Screen, where we experience the present moment and the things and relationships that give us life, and a Side Screen where we can view the fears, worries, and unhealthy temptations that vie for our attention. The point is to deliberately turn our attention to the Front Screen while leaving our worries behind on the Side Screen until it is time to deal with them directly.[19]

More information is available from his book and from a recorded talk he gave at an event sponsored by the Center for Faith and Enterprise.[20]

Religious and Spiritual Aspects

There is a long tradition of people finding relief from stress in their faith. In the Bible, this is frequently expressed in terms of faith in God, for example:

> *I will both lie down and sleep in peace;*
> *for you alone, O LORD, make me lie down in safety.*
> *Psalm 4:8*

> *Those of steadfast mind you keep in peace—*
> *in peace because they trust in you.*

Trust in the LORD forever,
for in the LORD God you have an everlasting rock.
Isaiah 26:3-4

Religion and spirituality can help in several different ways. These can include social support from pastors and members of the congregation; using religious attributions that help us find and maintain hope in the midst of stress; and the psychological benefits of practices like prayer, worship, ritual, and meditation that help calm and refocus us.

But there might also be possible downsides to religious coping. Psychologist Kenneth Pargament, in his book *The Psychology of Religion and Coping: Theory, Research, Practice*, observes that while religion can provide relief during times of stress, the actual form and content of religious coping is important. According to Pargament:

> The seemingly straightforward question, 'Does religion work,' could not be answered with a simple 'yes' or 'no.' Instead, the answer depends on the kind of religion one is talking about, who is doing the religious coping, and the situation the person is coping with. Depending on the interplay among these variables, religion can be helpful, harmful, or irrelevant to the coping process.[21]

It stands to reason that our concept of God is important. When God is understood as benevolent, religious coping methods are more likely to be helpful in terms of both reducing stress and constructively engaging the problem. I doubt the same would be true if we see God as primarily either judgmental or aloof, though, as Pargament points out, more research is needed.

––––––––––

Pargament suggests that there are three distinct types of religious coping. He describes them like this: "(1) the self-directing approach, wherein people rely on themselves in coping rather than on God; (2) the deferring approach, in which responsibility for coping is passively deferred to God; and(3) the collaborative approach, in which the individual and God are both active partners in coping."[22]

When coping with stressful events, I believe our primary goal should usually be to engage the problem constructively. Spiritual practices that promote constructive engagement are more likely to have positive outcomes in most situations than pain-avoidance strategies and are also more likely to result in lower levels of distress.

There are, of course, exceptions, such as circumstances in which we are faced with a threat about which we can do nothing (such as waiting for medical test results or the actions of others). Sometimes all we can do is wait and pray. And lowering the emotional and psychological pain associated with stress is not unimportant; reducing the pain can remove significant distractions that obstruct our effectiveness and damage our health and well-being.

But in my experience, stressful events in business more often than not confront us with a problem to be faced or solved. Engaging the problem, as in Pargament's collaborative approach, is usually the most likely to be successful in these cases. This can call for spiritual practices that help us stay spiritually connected as we engage the problem.

When looking for spiritual practices to help us deal with these situations, our objective is to identify ones that can: 1) help us stay calm psychologically, emotionally, and physically so that distractions are minimized; 2) lead us into a stance of constructive engagement; and 3) encourage a sense of spiritual connection that can both energize us and allow the crisis to become a source of spiritual growth.

Chapter Six contains examples of spiritual practices that can be quite useful when dealing with stress. Each involves some form of prayer.

———

As I said above, people in the Bible often dealt with stress by turning toward God in prayer and worship and believing that God was with them. Psalm 46 is an example of this. When I read it, I imagine the people of Israel facing a grave threat, perhaps an invading army outside the walls; they come together and chant the Psalm as a prayer, finding new courage as they do so. As you read it, you might listen for the emotions that are behind the words.

God is our refuge and strength,
  a very present help in trouble.
Therefore, we will not fear, though the earth should
    change,
  though the mountains shake in the heart of the sea;
  though its waters roar and foam,
  though the mountains tremble with its tumult.
    (Selah)

There is a river whose streams make glad the city of
    God,
  the holy habitation of the Most High.
God is in the midst of the city; it shall not be moved;
  God will help it when the morning dawns.
The nations are in an uproar, the kingdoms totter;
  he utters his voice, the earth melts.
The LORD of hosts is with us;
  the God of Jacob is our refuge. (Selah)

Come, behold the works of the LORD;
  see what desolations he has brought on the earth
He makes wars cease to the end of the earth;
  he breaks the bow, and shatters the spear;
  he burns the shields with fire.
"Be still, and know that I am God!
  I am exalted among the nations,
  I am exalted in the earth."

The LORD of hosts is with us;
  the God of Jacob is our refuge. (Selah)[23]
                                        Psalm 46

The people were probably experiencing the high stress associated with danger and possibly chaos, but their worship of God provided an anchor, a point of permanence and stillness. The culture and circumstances were undoubtedly very different from ours but maybe there is still something here that can speak to us in our situation. We too want to find a spiritual anchor amidst the tumult.

Our faith and spirituality might not solve or remove the stressful problems we are facing, but they might help us find the strength and wisdom necessary to engage the problems more productively and with less emotional wear and tear.

Work-Related Burnout

Work-related burnout is a big problem. Even if you have not experienced it yourself, you might in the future, and in any case, you probably know somebody who is confronting it right now.

In work-related small group discussions, I have pointed to Elijah in the wilderness as an example of burnout. Here is my adaptation of the story; maybe it will remind you of your own experience in some way.

> *After a prolonged struggle with King Ahab and the priests of Baal, the great prophet Elijah was completely exhausted. He journeyed by himself into the desert and asked God to take his life; he then lay down under a broom tree and fell asleep, awaiting death. Elijah's friends and allies were gone, he had failed to save Israel, and he was too tired to go on.*
>
> *But an angel sent by God awoke Elijah and gave him food and drink. After more rest, the angel brought Elijah to Mount Horeb to meet God in a cave.*
>
> *While at the cave, Elijah experienced a great wind, a powerful earthquake, and fire, but did not hear God. After these, he encountered sheer silence; within this silence, he heard God's voice. This gave him new confidence and a sense of mission and sent him back out to fulfill his calling.*
>
> *And so Elijah, refreshed, returned with power to the world and indeed fulfilled his calling from God.*
>
> *Adapted from 1 Kings 19:1-18*

From our vantage point, it is easy to see Elijah as an extreme case of work-related burnout. He was exhausted, he was without friends, and he felt like a purposeless failure. Maybe you have experienced something like this yourself; I certainly have.

Before we discuss how Elijah found renewal, let's look more closely at the nature of work-related burnout.

––––––––

Psychologists Christina Maslach and Michael P. Leiter wrote an important book called *The Truth About Burnout: How Organizations Cause Personal Stress and What To Do About It*. They talk about burnout like this:

> What might happen if you begin to burn out?
> Actually, three things happen: you become chronically
> exhausted; you become cynical and detached from
> your work; and you feel increasingly ineffective on the
> job.[24]

In other words, Maslach and Leiter have identified three essential characteristics, all of which need to be present for the condition to be classified as burnout. To resummarize these:

- **Chronic exhaustion:** This is not just the sort of tiredness we feel after working hard and for long hours over an extended period. This constant exhaustion stays with us and always seems to be there, even after rest.
- **Cynicism:** Some people might call this depersonalization. Our work no longer seems to have meaning for us. And this can apply to our working relationships as well; we can feel detached and disconnected from the people with whom we work.
- **Inefficacy:** We feel ineffective and powerless, and this generally prevents us from experiencing a sense of accomplishment.

Burnout is, in many ways, the opposite of active engagement. Instead of feeling energetic, involved, and productive, we feel exhausted, uninvolved, and unproductive. We can certainly see this in the case of Elijah.

It can result from severe and prolonged stress, including interpersonal stress. This stress usually results from the interaction between the individual and their work or their working environment. The dynamics can be quite complex; different individuals react to different stressors in different ways.

Maslach and Leiter suggest that burnout is often the result of a long-term mismatch between the individual and either the work or the environment. They describe several types of common mismatches;[25] I would describe some of them as follows:

- There can be a mismatch between the job requirements and the skills and resources brought to the job by the individual. In some cases, the individual might not have the skills necessary to do the work in a reasonably efficient and productive manner. Or, increasingly in today's workplace, the individual might be overloaded—he or she might have more work than they can get done. In either case, the result can be a feeling of chronic overwork.
- The mismatch can involve our values. The work might seem to require the individual to do something that does not sit well with them. Or it could be a situation where one feels like they are spending all of their time and energy on something quite different from what they believe is their true calling. This can lead the individual to ask the question, "Is this really what I am meant to do with my life?" It can become a very distressing situation.
- The mismatch can be interpersonal. For example, the individual might have trouble getting along with their boss or perhaps another coworker.
- A common form is when a person is working quite hard and believes they are performing well, but does not feel they are being compensated fairly, monetarily or in terms of respect and recognition. The feeling of being mistreated can be quite harmful, especially if it is allowed to continue over a significant period.
- A particularly troublesome situation can be where the work puts high demands on the individual, but the individual is not given adequate control over how to meet these demands.

Each of these mismatches can create a great deal of stress that seems to grind us down over time until we burn out.

Quite often, it seems that the people who had been the most passionate about their work, and maybe even had been the best performers, are also the ones most subject to the risk of burnout. We discussed Robert Vallerand's work on the two types of passion earlier. For our purposes here, the key point is that obsessive passion, with its compulsive quality and its tendency to be driven by extrinsic or defensive factors such as fear, a need to prove ourselves to others, or a feeling that our job is at risk, can readily lead to burnout.

What Can We Do About Burnout?

Maslach and Leiter, and other researchers, believe that situational and organizational problems are most often the cause of burnout.[26] While I would think that personal factors can also play a role, it makes sense to me that correcting the organizational problems is often the most important step. Those of us in a position of responsibility in our organization should be alert to possible sources of burnout and take corrective measures as appropriate. We need to be especially alert to people who are being worn down by mismatches with their work or working environment; this can be very important in the lives of the people involved. It can also be essential for the effectiveness of the organization.

But what if one cannot change the organization or the objective nature of the work? What can we do if we are the individual facing the potential of burnout?

There might be times when we need to consider changing jobs; this is something about which I cannot offer an opinion. There might also be times when professional help is needed; I am not qualified to express an opinion on this either. In the meantime, there are other things that seem to represent common sense when faced with burnout.

First, we might be able to strengthen our psychological and emotional resilience. Physical health can be important for this; adequate exercise, proper food, and enough sleep can help keep up our mental and physical energy (note that the angel first provided rest and food for Elijah). Strong, supportive interpersonal relationships are also important, whether they are within the workplace or without. These can help us build resilience and can buffer us from some of the emotional effects of stress.

Leisure time is especially important. Stepping away from our work and leaving our work identity behind allows us time to recover from workplace stress and reverse the depletion of our inner resources. There seems to be a sort of natural inner healing that occurs when we allow ourselves to be absorbed by an interest or an activity that is different from our work. Even a few minutes of rest in the middle of the workday can be helpful, though we should not lose sight of the fact that we also need more prolonged periods away.

But while leisure is important, the truth is that the very times when we are most in need of recovery also tend to be the times when it is most challenging to avail ourselves of the benefits of leisure. There may be times when we do not feel we can afford to take time off work. And there may be other times when we can take time off, but we are too busy ruminating about our work to enjoy the time away. Many of us have to work at relaxing; we need the recovery time, especially when we are facing burnout.

These points might sound obvious, and maybe they are, but we should keep in mind that when people are dealing with burnout, they are quite often in a sort of burnout-induced fog. They might be unable to see what would normally be considered obvious opportunities for rejuvenation, like social support and exercise.

Your Faith or Spirituality Can Help

One key to renewal might be in the resources of our faith or spirituality. Churches and other religious entities can provide a supportive community; strong personal relationships can help us build resilience and deal with some of the emotional effects of stress and burnout. Reading and reflecting on scripture and its connection with our daily life can help; the Bible contains many examples of people who have faced difficult times and from whom we can draw lessons. By its nature, the Bible directs our attention toward the eternal, the transcendent, and this by itself might help put our current challenges into a proper perspective.

As with stress, the spiritual or contemplative practices, such as prayer, some forms of worship, and prayerful meditation, might be helpful. There is something about turning our attention toward God in prayer that can connect us with a deep source of strength and wisdom. This can renew and energize us and help us develop a more profound sense of mission and purpose. It can also help us stay calm in times of crisis.

This seems to have been the case with Elijah. While the sleep and the food and drink provided by the angel certainly helped, it was really the experience of connection with God, hearing the quiet voice in the sheer silence, that was his real source of renewal and strength. Hearing the voice of God in the silence reconnected the great Elijah to the source of all power and meaning and love. It renewed him and sent him back into the world with the strength and courage he needed to fulfill his calling. Perhaps spiritual practices can help us in this way, too, if we pay attention.

Interpersonal Conflict

There is very little that will disrupt shalom as much as interpersonal conflict. Painfully difficult working relationships can harm our productivity, destroy collaboration, and distract us even when we are away from work. And they make us miserable. You may have seen this for yourself.

> *Better is a dry morsel with quiet*
> *than a house full of feasting with strife.*
> *Proverbs 17:1*

On the other hand, you may also have experienced the joy of reconciliation that sometimes comes after a personal conflict has been resolved. Many of us have experienced this as well.

While sin might play a role in interpersonal conflict, this is not always the primary or even a secondary cause. Sometimes the conflict is brought about by the fact we have goals that conflict with those of our coworkers. I do not have much to say about this, other than that we can be helped by staying calm, engaging in prayer, and maintaining an attitude of goodwill. We can also remember that the other person is also made in the image of God and might have a valid point of view.

But conflict and difficult working relationships are not always based on conflicting goals; the fact is that some people just annoy us (and we annoy them, in all likelihood) and this makes working together frustrating and challenging. We might try to suppress our annoyance, but sometimes it escapes into the open and makes things worse.

> *A soft answer turns away wrath,*
> *but a harsh word stirs up anger.*
>
> Proverbs 15:1

> *Those who are hot-tempered stir up strife,*
> *but those who are slow to anger calm*
> *contention.*
>
> Proverbs 15:18

Psychologist Sam Alibrando has spent decades helping people deal with interpersonal conflict. Because of the importance of his work on this issue, we arranged for the Center for Faith and Enterprise to invite Alibrando to speak at one of our Work Life Forums and are also working with him to produce new curriculum.[27]

Alibrando believes our more difficult working relationships are often caused by our reaction to differences in the emotional makeup of the two individuals involved and the imbalances these reactions create. To help understand this, he speaks in terms of an emotional triad (he credits several theorists for this concept, among them Wilfred Bion, Elias Porter, and especially Karen Horney). This triad consists of three categories or, as he calls them, dimensions of emotion:

- **Heart:** This involves reaching out to other people and trying to build positive relationships. Karen Horney calls this *moving toward* others.
- **Power:** This is when we act on behalf of our own interests or ideas; this can, at times, be in opposition to the interests or ideas of others. It is not necessarily negative; self-assertion can lead to the creation of new value and prosperity. Horney calls this *moving against* others.

- **Knowing:** This represents a combination of thinking and observation as we step back from the situation and disengage emotionally. Horney refers to this as *moving away*.

There can be both positive and negative aspects to each of these. For example, moving toward can lead to greater cooperation and an active concern for other people; on the other hand, it can also lead to too much dependency on others' opinions or approval. Moving against can be a useful frame of mind when we are promoting an important new idea or facing unreasonable resistance or opposition, but it can also result in ignoring the opinions of others, being blind to new input, or acting with malice. Moving away can result in new insights as we rethink the situation, but it can also manifest itself in disengagement and disinterest.

Difficult working relationships are most likely to arise when one person's emotional makeup triggers the other person's negative response, whether moving toward, against, or away. When this occurs, the relationship tends to become unbalanced. We are likely to become annoyed and see each other as difficult.

For example, a very assertive person (power/moving against) might have a tendency to run over a more quietly thoughtful person (knowing/moving away), creating resentment and a dysfunctional working relationship.

For Alibrando, the key to managing a difficult relationship is to manage ourselves and our emotions first. Understanding our emotional tendencies and those of other people can help us understand how to respond—rather than react—to people we might otherwise find difficult.

Managing ourselves is not necessarily easy; it requires us to develop emotional and spiritual strength. We also need to be able to see the relationship from the other person's point of view.

Here, too, our spirituality can help. It can help us remember the other person has inherent dignity and is worthy of love and respect, no matter the circumstances. It can help us be aware of the need for reconciliation as a key aspect of shalom. It can help us adopt prayer and other spiritual practices that help us calm down and be alert to what is going on around us and with other people. And it can help us develop the strength and patience to work through these problems.

We can also hope to develop a positive appreciation for the many differences between individuals and how in combination they make life more interesting and contribute to the blossoming of our culture.

Chapter Five

Cultivating Character Strengths

Virtues and character strengths (I will use these synonymously) help us overcome adversity, resist the temptations of sin, and deal with crises. They provide a foundation for shalom, form the basis for more productive collaborative relationships, and enhance our ability to meet our objectives and contribute to the well-being of society.

Perhaps most importantly, they help us stay spiritually grounded and act with integrity, courage, and purpose.

Before discussing the various virtues and character strengths, I would like to tell a story.

A few years ago, I attended a dinner meeting on faith and work organized by a church. After dinner, the organizer asked us to go around the table and discuss the issues we face in our work. One young manager spoke up and complained that he was having a difficult time balancing his desire for success with his attempt to live by the virtues taught by his church, especially honesty and fair dealing. His comment surprised me, so I spoke with him afterward and challenged him a bit. He was insistent, however, that in his industry, his desire to maintain his integrity was getting in the way of his ambitions.

This bothered me, so I thought about it for a few days. As I did so, I realized that while I did not know his situation, in every business and industry in which I have worked, if you lost your reputation for honesty and fair dealing, you would find it very difficult to do business with other people and would probably find it hard to be successful as a result.

There is a false ideology at work in the world: the idea that the virtues promoted by churches and other religious entities are in fundamental conflict with business effectiveness and the success we hope to achieve. This false ideology seems to underpin much of what we hear from outside commentators when the topic of business comes up.

Collaboration and the Values and Virtues We Bring to Our Work

The virtues taught by churches and other religious institutions, such as humility, compassion, honesty, transparency, equanimity, and courage, are essential in their own right, but they are also highly important in our work lives.

In business and related vocations, effectiveness is heavily dependent on collaboration and healthy collaborative relationships, in other words, on the building of community. And healthy collaborative relationships are, in turn, dependent on the virtues taught by most religious traditions.

Nobody wants to do business with someone they cannot trust. It is very hard to form a productive working relationship if there is no mutual concern for each other's well-being. It is also tough to work productively with someone who is narcissistic and has little or no sense of humility. An organization that mistreats its employees will have a hard time generating trust and voluntary cooperation.

There are, of course, exceptions. We can all point to someone who seems to be low on the integrity scale, or perhaps routinely mistreats coworkers and employees, but nevertheless seems to be getting ahead. But I believe these really are the exceptions. Mistreating others usually makes it harder, not easier, to meet one's business objectives.

Much of the value of collaboration and collaborative relationships is derived from the nature of business itself. To be clear, when I talk about business, I am not talking about things like political cronyism or the attempt to tie up scarce resources in order to charge above-market prices. When I speak of business, I mean the creative, productive process of producing value in the form of goods and services that others want to buy. It is this creative, productive process that most calls for collaboration.

Virtually any product or service we can find on the market has a vast network of activities behind it, all of which involve collaborative relationships. Of course, there is often an element of negotiation concerning prices, delivery schedules, etc. And competition between alternative vendors undoubtedly comes into play. Nevertheless, the network of productive activity is grounded primarily in collaboration and collaborative relationships. It is mainly our working relationships that determine our success, not our willingness to engage in cutthroat competition.

And yet we occasionally hear religious and other commentators complain about the alienation and isolation of the individual brought about by modern business culture. Rather than understanding success as mostly the result of productive collaboration, the false ideology promoted by these commentators sees business as being driven by obsessive greed, uncontrolled narcissism, and competitive ruthlessness. Sometimes commercially successful people reinforce this attitude by using expressions like "giving back," as though they built their success on "taking" rather than on producing and giving.

Some people unfortunately buy into this ideology, apparently including the people who influenced the young manager in the above story. I would not bet on the long-term prospects of a business with the values he described.

The truth is that most people who have been in business or related occupations for a few years have learned that without treating people properly, it is difficult, if not impossible, to form the collaborative relationships usually necessary for success. There are certainly moral lapses, and we have each stumbled, but these lapses typically lead to lower, not higher, levels of effectiveness despite what we might hear about presumed trade-offs between success and integrity, or between profits and people.

A Spiritual Connection?

Character strengths not only play an instrumental role in our work by promoting collaboration and shalom, they can also help us resist the pressures of the workplace so that we can be true to our authentic selves and our deeper purpose. By keeping our more negative motivations under control, we can allow our better selves to come to the surface and be expressed through our work.

We can see hints of a connection between our spirituality and our character strengths (or lack thereof) in the Bible. God hardens Pharaoh's heart so he cannot act wisely in his dealings with Moses. God gives King Saul an evil spirit that creates in him fear, anxiety, and foolishness. Solomon was given wisdom by God, at least in the early years of his reign. Others were given a spirit of courage and wisdom. God's Holy Spirit provided individuals with hope, courage, patience, and compassion.

There might be something deeper and more mysterious going on here. I believe that when the Bible says that God gave someone a spirit of a particular type, this speaks to the common intuition that there is a connection between spirituality and character. In our own lives, we might have experienced the feeling that acting on one of these strengths (such as humility, compassion, or integrity) seemed to open us to God or other people in some way. People of almost all religious views see spirituality as having to do with being a better person; perhaps our intuitions are pointing toward a connection we cannot quite see.

Conversely, when our character strengths weaken, when we succumb to temptation and experience moral failure, or when our courage fails us, it is easy to feel spiritually adrift and disconnected from the deeper meaning of our work. When it comes to character, we have each experienced both strengths and weaknesses. We are a mixture of both.

Fortunately, there is reason to believe we can develop character strengths over time and that our faith or spirituality can help. Professor of psychology Matthew Rossano thinks that what he calls moral expertise can be developed, and that while religion may not be necessary for this, religious participation can help in several ways. Religions usually promote moral standards, point to exemplars from whom we can learn, call for self-critical reflection, and provide opportunities and encouragement for moral action.[28]

I would add that our faith or spirituality can help us see the deeper meaning in our work and be more alert to the positive and negative consequences of our actions. And spiritual practices can help us strengthen our will and develop perspective. These can help us develop each of the strengths discussed later in this chapter.

Types of Strengths

Character strengths are intertwined with shalom and our relationship to God throughout the Bible. Christian theology does not say that good character and virtuous behavior earn us a place in heaven, nor do they guarantee good results in our lives; good people can and do suffer. But good character, as lived out through our behavior, does tend to lead toward a better life—toward shalom.

The Bible contains a collection of proverbs that provide advice for life and work; such collections were not uncommon in the Ancient Near East. These place special emphasis on character strengths and the associated behavior. For example:

> *Like a city breached, without walls,*
> *is one who lacks self-control.*
> *Proverbs 25:28*

> *The appetite of the lazy craves, and gets nothing,*
> *while the appetite of the diligent is richly supplied.*
> *Proverbs 13:4*

> *By insolence the heedless make strife,*
> *but wisdom is with those who take advice.*
> *Proverbs 13:10*

> *The integrity of the upright guides them,*
> *but the crookedness of the treacherous destroys them.*
> *Proverbs 11:3*

> *One who forgives an affront fosters friendship,*
> *but one who dwells on disputes will alienate a friend.*
> *Proverbs 17:9*

> *One who spares words is knowledgeable;*
> *one who is cool in spirit has understanding.*

Even fools who keep silent are considered wise;
when they close their lips, they are deemed intelligent.
Proverbs 17:27-28

Contemporary research psychologists have provided useful categorizations and descriptions of virtues and character strengths. Christopher Peterson and Martin Seligman listed twenty-four character strengths in their book *Character Strengths and Virtues: A Handbook and Classification.* They organized these into six summary virtues: wisdom and knowledge, courage, humanity, justice, temperance, and transcendence.[29] These are quite similar to what we see in the Bible, though without the religious orientation.

Psychologist Angela Duckworth organizes character strengths a little differently and puts them into three categories: strengths of heart that encourage harmonious interpersonal relationships, strengths of mind, and strengths of will.[30]

Character strengths in each of these categories are essential for shalom. They are each frequently mentioned in the Bible, and I would say their development can benefit from prayer, meditation, and self-discipline.

Of the three, I think we are most likely to overlook the contribution to spiritual growth of the strengths of mind category (or intellect). A couple of years ago, I met with a friend who is a highly dedicated, and successful, scientist. I asked him if he saw a connection between his work and faith, and he immediately said yes. In his view, God created reality and therefore we should learn as much about it as we can. I wish more of us found such a sense of joy and purpose in our intellectual activity and our work overall; I came away inspired.

We cannot cover all the character strengths identified by Peterson, Seligman, and Duckworth, but we will focus on seven that are especially important in our work. These are integrity, courage, compassion/kindness, humility, prudence, resilience, and hope.

Integrity

Integrity is one of the most important virtues. Before we discuss integrity, however, I have to say that I am usually somewhat reluctant to talk about it; sometimes it seems as though we are always being preached at about integrity and morality—what more could possibly be said? It is also easy to feel hypocritical when we talk about integrity; we are probably each well aware of when we have fallen short, and how often.

Yet it is an important subject, and I think a story from the book of Genesis about Joseph and Potiphar's wife might have some valuable insights for us. In the run-up to the part that I include below, Joseph is sold into slavery by his older brothers. Potiphar, a prominent Egyptian official, buys Joseph and puts him to work. Potiphar is so impressed by Joseph that he makes him the overseer of his house and his fields.

Then trouble emerges. Try to put yourself in Joseph's position as you read the rest of the story:

> *Now Joseph was handsome and good-looking. And after a time his master's wife cast her eyes on Joseph and said, "Lie with me." But he refused and said to his master's wife, "Look, with me here, my master has no concern about anything in the house, and he has put everything that he has in my hand. He is not greater in this house than I am, nor has he kept back anything from me except yourself, because you are his wife. How then could I do this great wickedness, and sin against God?" And although she spoke to Joseph day after day, he would not consent to lie beside her or to be with her.*
>
> *One day, however, when he went into the house to do his work, and while no one else was in the house, she caught hold of his garment, saying, "Lie with me!" But he left his garment in her hand, and fled and ran outside.*
>
> *When she saw that he had left his garment in her hand and had fled outside, she called out to the members of her household and said to them, "See, my husband has brought among us a Hebrew to insult us! He came in to me to lie with me, and I cried out with a loud voice; and when he heard me raise my voice and cry out, he left his garment beside me, and fled outside." Then she kept his*

> *garment by her until his master came home, and she told*
> *him the same story . . .*
> *When his master heard the words that his wife spoke*
> *to him, saying, "This is the way your servant treated*
> *me," he became enraged. And Joseph's master took him*
> *and put him into the prison, the place where the king's*
> *prisoners were confined; Joseph remained there in prison.*
> *But the LORD was with Joseph and showed him*
> *steadfast love; he gave him favor in the sight of the chief*
> *jailer. So the chief jailer committed to Joseph's care all*
> *the prisoners who were in the prison, and whatever was*
> *done there, Joseph was the one who did it. The chief*
> *jailer paid no heed to anything that was in Joseph's care,*
> *because the LORD was with Joseph; and whatever he*
> *did, the LORD made it prosper.*
>
> *Genesis 39: 6-23*

What did doing the right thing cost Joseph? At first glance, it cost him just about everything—his job, his material well-being, his status, and his safety.

But did he not also gain something—perhaps something having to do with integrity?

People often think of integrity as "doing the right thing," and this is generally true. But more specifically, integrity has to do with alignment; it means our values, beliefs, and actions are all aligned. Sometimes we speak of our words and actions, or our beliefs and our actions, as being consistent. Some would say our actions match our words.

With integrity, there is a unity to who we are and how we act. This involves acting in accord with our true selves and has a spiritual dimension. When we act with integrity, our authentic self is expressed through our words and our actions.

At the end of the story, note that despite Joseph's low standing and his apparent criminality, the jailer saw something special in him, leading the jailer to put great trust in Joseph. The same goes for Potiphar at the beginning of the story. Some might say that what Potiphar and the jailer saw was Joseph's intelligence, but I think it was actually his integrity as they saw the way Joseph behaved.

There is something about integrity, about being in alignment, that seems to help us think more clearly and act with more power. When we are acting in alignment with our true selves, we spend less energy on inner conflict and negative internal conversations. We are able to act with greater wisdom, purpose, and power.

Sometimes others can see this. Joseph had integrity and it led people to entrust him with more and more responsibility, even to the point, several years after this story, that Joseph became one of the most powerful people in Egypt.

There are no guarantees. Circumstances over which we have no control can overwhelm us, whether we have integrity or not. We also make mistakes, sometimes well-meaning mistakes. Nothing, not even integrity, can guarantee success or even survival.

But integrity can at least provide a foundation for weathering the storm and maybe rising again. We have each fallen short, far short and more often than we like to admit. But we can still endeavor to act with integrity in the present and in the future.

In the pressured and sometimes barely controlled chaos of the workplace, there can be a temptation to respond, or to over-respond, to social pressure and to act falsely. Integrity helps us to push back against these pressures and maintain our authenticity.

This is not always easy, especially when challenges to our integrity emerge suddenly, before we are ready and without warning. To prepare for these challenges, there are two questions you might want to ask yourself:

> What are the challenges to your integrity you are most likely to encounter at work?

> What are you prepared to sacrifice for the sake of your integrity?

Thinking seriously about these two questions might help you prepare for the challenges that could come your way.

Institutional Integrity

The preceding applies primarily to individual integrity as it pertains to our work and our business relationships. In these situations, it is easy to see how integrity applies to individuals. But what about organizations?

There sometimes seems to be an institutional dynamic that can override individual ethics. Imagine if an executive of a social media company was your neighbor; what would be the likelihood that he or she would sneak into your house and secretly plant software in your smartphone that would track your movements and shopping behavior without you knowing about it? Pretty close to zero. But for some reason, when thinking institutionally, some people are willing to do things that they would never countenance in their personal relationships.

Other examples of institutional malfeasance might include a tech company that provides dictators with software that can be used for the suppression of human rights in exchange for market access; governmental bodies and political organizations that run up massive, unsustainable levels of debt that they know will eventually lead to catastrophe; and nonprofits that knowingly mislead their donors in order to raise more money for their good cause. How do otherwise ethical people find themselves in these situations?

Management scholars Elizabeth Umphress and John Bingham coined the expression "unethical pro-organizational behavior" (U.P.B.) for:

> ... actions that are intended to promote the effective functioning of the organization or its members (e.g., leaders) and violate core societal values, mores, laws, or standards of proper conduct.[31]

Social relationships and strong organizational identity seem to be key factors. Umphress and Bingham point to the ethical environment of the organization and the person's loyalty to it. If an organization appears to allow particular forms of bad behavior that seem to benefit the organization, at least in the short run, then they are likely to get more of it. As people become socialized into an organizational context, their own ethical standards can be overlooked or neutralized.

A friend who was the C.F.O. of a $10 billion company periodically spoke to groups of new hires of his company and told them they must not do anything of an illegal, immoral, or unethical nature, even if they thought it was in support of the company's objectives. If they did so, the company would disavow their actions and terminate their employment. He believed, as do I, that organizations need to send a strong and visible message against such behavior; the temptations and potential for misunderstanding may otherwise cause serious problems.

I do not think the primary cause of institutional moral failure is necessarily the personal financial interest of the decision-makers. A more likely explanation is that when we think of the well-being of others, we naturally think of the people we know, which in the case of a large institution, usually means the people with whom we work. We therefore have a natural inclination to see the greater good in terms of the well-being of the institution.

Many of the people who make these kinds of decisions probably think of themselves as moral and normally behave with as much integrity in their personal lives as the rest of us. But they can be tempted to make decisions that benefit their organization in ways that require overlooking what would otherwise be their moral standards. And this is not just the leaders. If all our working relationships, or at least the dominant ones, are with people inside the organization, then the social pressure can be intense, and the temptations great, to take care of the institution, our team, first.

The prophets of the Bible stood up against this sort of social pressure. Their mission was to speak what they believed to be the word of God to their society as it was moving in the wrong direction, and to do so despite the social and political pressure. These were brave, courageous people. We need to develop the same sort of courage and clear-headed integrity, and I believe our faith or spirituality can play a key role in this. Reading and reflecting on the stories in the Bible about people who faced similar or greater challenges can help us keep our eyes open and our courage up.

Courage

We each face fears, anxieties, and stresses in our work lives, and a great deal of attention has been given to the question of how we can better cope with or ameliorate these feelings. But what if we turned the question around?

What if instead of asking how can we cope better, we asked how can we develop and act with more courage despite our fears?

It is not that learning to cope with negative emotions is never appropriate; there are certainly times when it is essential. But I believe in many cases we have over-emphasized passive coping skills and neglected the need to act courageously despite our fear and anxiety.

––––––––––

Courage has been an admired virtue for as long as we humans have walked the earth. It is valued by virtually every human culture.

We see this as far back as the Epic of Gilgamesh—widely regarded as the earliest known written story, from more than 4,000 years ago. The courage of Gilgamesh is critical as the story unfolds. We also see the value of courage in the ancient Greek stories and in other ancient cultures.

And we see it in the Bible. For example, as the Israelites prepare to cross the Jordan River and face their enemies, Joshua tells the people three times: "be strong and courageous" (Joshua 1:6, 7, 9). When King David is on his deathbed, he gives final instructions to his son Solomon; these include the admonition to "be strong and be courageous" (1 Kings 2:2). And this advice appears again in a vision given to Daniel, when the angel tells him of future conflicts and chaos and advises Daniel to "be strong and courageous" (Daniel 10:19).

These heroes were not just trying to cope with fear or mitigate its pain. They were trying to summon the courage they needed to push through their fear and overcome their obstacles.

Courage is also important in our work lives. We need to think clearly, make calm, reasoned decisions, and take the actions needed. This often takes courage.

Individual courage in the face of social pressure is essential for the long-term health of organizations. Think of the individual who openly opposes the direction of the group or organization and does so despite considerable social pressure and risk to his or her job or status. This could involve taking a stand against some aspect of the organization's activity, or perhaps disagreeing with an impending decision or strategy. There are times when institutional integrity depends on the courage of an individual taking a stand in the face of social or institutional pressure.

Organizational behavior scholars Fred Luthans, Carolyn Youssef, and Bruce Avolio note that courage is not just for "extraordinary situations characterized by extremely high risks," but for more ordinary situations as well.[32] Courage is often essential for getting things done in the workplace.

What Do We Mean By Courage?

Peterson and Seligman spoke of courage as follows:

> Strengths of courage entail the exercise of will to accomplish goals in the face of opposition, either external or internal.[33]

They go on to associate four particular strengths with the virtue of courage. As you would guess, the first is bravery, which involves facing and not shrinking from a threat. This often includes physical bravery, but not always. The second is persistence; this is a matter of continuing on a course of action despite the obstacles. The third is integrity, which means speaking the truth and presenting oneself authentically, without subterfuge.

The fourth strength, and the one that surprised me, is vitality, by which they mean "approaching life with excitement and energy; *not* doing things halfway or halfheartedly; living life as an adventure; feeling fully alive and activated." They point out that it is difficult to act courageously if we do not have vitality, what I would call positive energy.[34]

Others have looked at courage in terms of the courageous act itself. Psychologist Christopher Rate, using research developed by his team (Jennifer Clarke, Douglas Lindsay, and Robert Sternberg) as well as that of others, proposed that an act of courage includes three essential elements:

> . . . (a) a willing, intentional act, (b) involving substantial danger, difficulty, or risk to the actor, (c) primarily motivated to bring about a noble good or morally worthy purpose.[35]

Psychologist Monica Worline found that most often "courage in organizations happens in the form of resisting conformity, seizing individual responsibility regardless of role, and challenging authority."[36] She speaks of individuals acting in "constructive opposition," in other words, on behalf of the collective good but in opposition to prevailing opinion or other pressure. Such acts can open new possibilities for consideration.[37]

Factors Contributing to Courage

Courage seems to come more naturally to some people. This could be the result of a combination of genetics, prior successful experience with courage, and the strength of one's motivation. And this can vary by the type of situation they face; think of the person who has exhibited outstanding personal bravery but is petrified when faced with speaking to a large crowd.

Nevertheless, there's ample reason to believe that courage can be developed. The following are some of the factors that are important; each of these can be cultivated through prayer, reflection, and practice.

Sense of Purpose:
A strong sense of purpose can provide the motivation to overcome our fears. While external incentives matter, having a sense of purpose that reflects our intrinsic values and drives—and that is expressed in the actions we are taking—can provide a deep sense of courage.

I believe the internal aspect of this is critical. We are usually much more motivated and better able to face obstacles and fears, if our sense of purpose comes from deep within us and expresses our true selves. External motivation (social pressure, desire for economic gain, etc.) can help, but cannot take the place of motivation that comes from within.

This is a spiritual matter for many people. Some might say that our deepest motivation reflects not just our true selves but the mysterious connection with God that is at the core of our being.

The Moral Foundation of Our Action:
In many biblical stories, the heroes believe that God is on their side and will support them if they are obedient; this belief makes it easier to act with courage.

I would not say that God guarantees our success or even stacks the deck in our favor. But there is still an important truth in the Biblical perspective: knowing we are doing the right thing, and acting in accord with our integrity and maybe even with what we believe to be the will of God, can be a source of confidence, strength, and wisdom. Being clear on why we are willing to face these challenges, and why it is the right thing to do, is essential.

The moral sense with which we act often includes altruism; many people find more courage when acting to help a vulnerable person in trouble.

Confidence, Agency, and Self-Efficacy:
People who act courageously are often more confident than other people. This can involve a high level of agency (belief in their ability to take intentional action) and self-efficacy (a belief in their effectiveness). A strong sense of agency and self-efficacy can be cultivated over time by accepting tasks and challenges that require us to develop new strengths. Our sense of confidence grows as we do so, and this confidence can extend to new challenges.[38]

Social Networks (Good and Bad):
There is plenty of evidence that having a strong, supportive social network can, in many situations, enhance our courage, especially if we are acting to protect our community. Cultivating supportive relationships can be very helpful.

Sometimes, however, we are required to act contrary to the opinion of others. Most of us have had the unpleasant experience of having to break bad news to a boss or customer, or speaking out against the consensus of the group. We have experienced the power of social pressure firsthand.

In these situations, our social context can work against courage, especially if our actions are likely to be unpopular. Social forces can even blind us to the moral issues involved in our situation. We need to cultivate the ability to think for ourselves.

One way to bridge these concerns is to have a support network outside of our work that we know will support our tough decisions no matter what. Such a group can strengthen our will when we need to go against the grain in our work setting.

Spiritual Practices:
Spiritual practices, such as prayer and meditation, can help us stay grounded, calm, and focused. They can also help us be aware of the spiritual dimension and our mission.

There are a great many practices from which to choose, such as a few minutes of meditative silence, a prayerful reflection on a passage of scripture, or a silent prayer. Chapter Six has more ideas.

Stories of Courage in the Bible

Studying exemplars who act with great courage can help us reflect on how we might share in such courage.

The Bible has a great many examples. We could think of the prophet Elijah doing battle with two hundred prophets of Baal, Jeremiah imprisoned in an underground cistern for speaking out against the authorities, Noah building the ark despite derision by his community, or Jesus facing torture and death at the hands of the religious establishment. These individuals each spoke the truth as they understood it, often in opposition to their community and while facing extreme duress.

The apostle Paul presents a vivid example of courage. Paul was a well-placed, up-and-coming member of the Pharisees until he had what the Bible describes as an encounter with the resurrected Jesus on the road to Damascus. Paul wound up opposing his Pharisaic community to proclaim the gospel and did so against what must have been intense social pressure. Because of his understanding of the gospel and his sense of calling, he then began spreading the news to non-Jews despite the opposition of much of the Christian leadership. In the process, he endured beatings, stoning, imprisonment, and eventually martyrdom.

For me, the most moving example of courage in the Bible is the story of Jesus in the garden of Gethsemane a short time before the arrest that led to his torture and death. Jesus asks three of his disciples to watch while he goes a little farther away and prays by himself. The disciples seem to be oblivious to the stress he is going through and repeatedly fall asleep.

Meanwhile, Jesus is beside himself with fear, even to the point of throwing himself on the ground. He prays: "Abba, Father, for you all things are possible; remove this cup from me." He does not want to go through what is in store for him (to drink from the cup that has been set before him). But he continues to pray and in prayer finds the strength he needs. He goes on to pray: "Yet, not what I want, but what you want."

Despite his fear, Jesus musters the extraordinary courage he needs to carry out his mission. And with that, he allows himself to be captured, tortured, and crucified (Mark 14:32-42).

———

Even if at first we only take small steps in the direction of being more courageous, I believe the benefits can be enormous.

Compassion (and Kindness)

We can define compassion as a deep, heartfelt concern for others, manifested in a willingness to help. It reflects our natural desire to contribute to the well-being of other people. Some experts distinguish between compassion and kindness, with compassion seen more narrowly as a response to suffering.[39] While I think that is valid, for our purposes here I will use the two synonymously.

The story of the Good Samaritan, as told by Jesus, might have some insights for us. Note that Jesus's audience would have had a low opinion of Samaritans. Yet it is a Samaritan in the story who comes to the aid of the beaten man.

> *Just then a lawyer stood up to test Jesus. "Teacher,"*
> *he said, "what must I do to inherit eternal life?" Jesus*
> *said to him, "What is written in the law? What do you*
> *read there?" He answered, "You shall love the Lord your*
> *God with all your heart, and with all your soul, and*
> *with all your strength, and with all your mind; and your*
> *neighbor as yourself." And Jesus said to him, "You have*
> *given the right answer; do this, and you will live."*

> *But wanting to justify himself, he asked Jesus, "And*
> *who is my neighbor?"*
> *Jesus replied, "A man was going down from Jerusalem*
> *to Jericho, and fell into the hands of robbers, who*
> *stripped him, beat him, and went away, leaving him half*
> *dead. Now by chance a priest was going down that road;*
> *and when he saw him, he passed by on the other side.*
> *So likewise a Levite, when he came to the place and saw*
> *him, passed by on the other side.*
> *"But a Samaritan while traveling came near him;*
> *and when he saw him, he was moved with pity. He went*
> *to him and bandaged his wounds, having poured oil*
> *and wine on them. Then he put him on his own animal,*
> *brought him to an inn, and took care of him. The next*
> *day he took out two denarii, gave them to the innkeeper,*
> *and said, 'Take care of him; and when I come back, I will*
> *repay you whatever more you spend.'*
> *"Which of these three, do you think, was a neighbor*
> *to the man who fell into the hands of the robbers?" He*
> *said, "The one who showed him mercy." Jesus said to*
> *him, "Go and do likewise."*
>
> *Luke 10:25-37*

There seems to be something about acting with compassion that has spiritual meaning. Perhaps we associate acts of kindness with the virtues advocated by the Bible and other religious traditions. Or maybe we experience a sense that God is acting through us in some way.

We would probably each agree that we should behave compassionately toward our fellow humans, whether at work or anywhere else; even the priest and the Levite in the story would probably agree. There are, however, times when we fall short and fail to act with an appropriate degree of compassion.

Quite often, our shortcomings in this area are not so much deliberate as they are a result of being preoccupied with other priorities. When working hard and focusing on the job at hand, it can be challenging to shift gears and give our attention to an issue that is unrelated to our task, even if the issue is a personal problem calling for our compassion. Moreover, it can be natural for us to filter out information not critical for the task, even important human signals that we would otherwise notice.

Psychologists Worline and Jane Dutton say that "noticing is the portal to awakening compassion at work" but this is "much harder than it seems."[40] In any sizable group of people, there are likely to be some who are suffering and not acknowledging it to others, though the pain might come out in anger, nervousness, or disengagement. Our ability to notice and respond to subtle clues can make an important difference in people's lives.

This can be especially difficult in virtual settings where people are less likely to bring their problems into the conversation. But noticing and taking action are important for the well-being of the people involved.

While the well-being of the individual is the most important consideration, there is also a secondary benefit for the organization. People who are carrying painful burdens unrecognized by their organization are not likely to be either loyal or productive. On the other hand, compassion can be a powerful builder of community and teamwork. Worline and Dutton discuss this secondary benefit:

> Because of its role in enhancing collective capabilities like innovation, service quality, collaboration, and adaptability, compassion matters for competitive advantage. Think of it this way: when human suffering threatens to diminish collective capabilities such as working together creatively and quickly, compassion restores and even strengthens the organization's ability to accomplish its aims.[41]

Are There Downsides to Compassion and Kindness at Work?

Sometimes people feel they need to apply different boundaries to their compassion in the workplace than in other areas of their life. We might have concerns that being too kind might lead others to take advantage of us or set a precedent we cannot maintain. We might also worry about not being able to hold people responsible for their work or their obligations to us.

There can indeed be times when people take unfair advantage of one's kindness, even to the point of putting others in an untenable position. While I do not believe that this is how most people behave, we need to be prepared to change direction as we learn more about the situation with which we are dealing.

There are also times when kindness cannot be the only criteria for making decisions. Business owners, managers, and others need to be mindful of all the people who rely on the business. The needs of employees must be balanced with the needs of customers, suppliers, owners, and investors. One cannot offer a level of employee benefits, for example, that puts the business's solvency at risk. That does not mean that the decision-making process needs to be seen as a zero-sum game; leaders can help organizations develop a sense of common purpose that provides an overarching criterion for decision-making and that takes into account the people who need our compassion.

We need to exercise judgment if we are to help people effectively. We also need to be open to new information and alert to the condition of the people with whom we work. Sometimes this means taking time to understand the situation before acting, though there are also times when immediate action is needed. It can be difficult to know what to do; sometimes considerable discernment is required.[42]

Developing Compassion

Some people are naturally more compassionate than others. This could be because of genetic inheritance, early childhood experiences, or development over the years.

I believe individuals can intentionallly develop more compassion. For example, we develop it by paying attention to others and by making sure we are open and willing to listen.

This is also an organizational issue. Tense, stressful environments are less likely to encourage compassion than are more positive environments. Reducing the stress level, and especially internal conflict and competition, can help—not that this is easy to do.

An organization that encourages openness, empathy, and acts of kindness is more likely to have employees who behave accordingly, especially if the leaders are positive examples of this behavior. Leaders would be wise to look for opportunities to set good examples.

In any case, we should treat others in the workplace compassionately because it is the right thing to do. Let's also remember that healthy, flourishing organizations require strong relationships that are hard to imagine without significant concern for each other's well-being.

> *Some give freely, yet grow all the richer;*
> *others withhold what is due, and only suffer want.*
> *A generous person will be enriched,*
> *and one who gives water will get water.*
> *The people curse those who hold back grain,*
> *but a blessing is on the head of those who sell it.*
>   Proverbs 11:24-26

Humility

Humility is usually treated as a virtue that should be cultivated for its own sake, whether it provides practical benefits or not. While I believe this to be true, I also think humility can also contribute to our spiritual and psychological flourishing, with significant benefits for our work.

Quite a few business leaders and management researchers have concluded that a leader's effectiveness is often closely associated with their humility.[43] While a narcissistic or prideful leader can sometimes project a charismatic image and attract followers, such leaders are much less likely to be effective over time than leaders with more humility. There are well-known exceptions, of course, and the expectations about leaders might vary by culture, but for the most part, humility is an important quality in leaders.

> *When pride comes, then comes disgrace;*
> *but wisdom is with the humble.*
>   Proverbs 11:2

A fool takes no pleasure in understanding,
but only in expressing personal opinion.
                                    Proverbs 18:2

Do you see persons wise in their own eyes?
There is more hope for fools than for them.
                                    Proverbs 26:12

Research psychologist and professor Robert Emmons points out that humility is sometimes equated with low self-regard, but genuine humility is different. It is "the realistic appraisal of one's strengths and weaknesses—neither overestimating them nor underestimating them."[44] This realism becomes more palatable as our concern for our self-worth decreases.

June Tangney, George Mason University professor, has identified six interrelated elements of humility, which I would summarize as follows: an accurate self-appraisal; a willingness to acknowledge one's limitations and mistakes; an openness to advice, new ideas, and contradictory information; a greater appreciation for other people and for what other people contribute; a realistic sense of perspective regarding one's own place in the world; and a relatively low self-focus.[45] We can see the common thread in these elements: humility allows one to be open to people and to the world and to take in more information. With humility, the defense of one's ego needs and social status does not get in the way of being open to new information and relationships.

Some elements within the Christian tradition have advocated different forms of self-abasement in the name of humility. Some religious devotees have tried to use self-abasement as a way to develop virtue or to stimulate spiritual experiences. That is not what we are talking about here.

I think the value of humility is quite apparent. If we look at it through a religious or spiritual lens, we can see that if we let go of our self-concern, we can be more open to reality. We will be more likely to hear and respond to the concerns of others. We will be more aware of our deep yearning for spiritual connection, purpose, and growth, and we will probably be more open to spiritual experience.

We can also look at humility through a business or organizational lens. In this case, we can see that if we are more open to information that has not been filtered through our own ego needs, we are more likely to see things as they are and act with wisdom. We are also more likely to appreciate other people and the contribution they make. And this is bound to lead to stronger relationships, greater collaboration, and more effective leadership.

Compare this to the prideful or narcissistic person who is so caught up in maintaining a high degree of self-importance and high social status that he or she cannot take in information that might not support their self-evaluation. Their pride might generate some motivation and confidence, which can be quite useful in some circumstances. But a reluctance to accept some types of ego-threatening information can also close the person off from the ideas of others and make it much more difficult to form effective working relationships.

In a business context where innovation and the ability to read the environment accurately can be critical to our survival, narcissism and excessive pride can be highly dysfunctional no matter how much so-called charisma is projected by the person involved.

No matter which of these lenses we apply, the spiritual or the business, it should be clear that by reducing our excessive self-concern, humility can help us engage life more deeply and help us be more fully alive, psychologically and spiritually. And this is bound to be enormously valuable in our daily lives and for the people with whom we come in contact.

Humility might be difficult to develop directly. Psychologist and researcher Peter Hill suggests that it might make more sense to focus on developing particular markers of humility. [46] These could include a stronger awareness of our own limitations, avoiding focusing on ourselves, and paying more attention to other people.

I would also suggest that religious or spiritual practices that take the focus off ourselves might be useful here; these can include worship, some forms of prayer, and scripture reading. A key might be to focus on God and other people and not on our own worthiness.

Prudence

The virtue of prudence is implicit in much of the Bible. It involves making good decisions that prioritize long-term goals and consequences; it also involves a willingness to resist short-term goals, desires, and impulses that interfere with the longer-term. This requires not just intelligence and knowledge but also self-control.

Long-term success often requires short-term sacrifice. This is not a new issue; the Bible spoke to this thousands of years ago:

> *Whoever loves pleasure will suffer want; whoever loves*
> *wine and oil will not be rich.*
>> *Proverbs 21:17*

> *Precious treasure remains in the house of the wise, but*
> *the fool devours it.*
>> *Proverbs 21:20*

Peterson and Seligman speak of prudence like this:

> Prudent individuals show a farsighted and deliberative
> concern for the consequences of their actions and deci-
> sions, successfully resist impulses and other choices
> that satisfy shorter term goals at the expense of longer
> term ones, have a flexible and moderate approach
> to life, and strive for balance among their goals and
> ends.[47]

We are frequently confronted with trade-offs between long-term goals and short-term benefits. An almost stereotypical case is that of the corporate manager who faces short-term pressure for quarterly profits and consequently does things that work against long-term objectives. I certainly experienced this in a corporate job several decades ago; while the company paid lip service to long-term strategic priorities, the real pressure was on meeting the short-term sales and profit commitments.

There are plenty of times when we need to sacrifice our short-term pleasure for the sake of our long-term goals. These sacrifices can come in many different forms; many of us, myself included, can be drawn to the work we enjoy to such an extent that we frequently neglect the types of necessary work that we do not like.

And this applies not only to the pursuit of wealth; the concept can apply to any conflict between short-term and long-term priorities. When the rewards do not arrive until well into the future, we are easily tempted away from what we should be doing, or to work on short-term priorities while rejecting more important long-term ones.

Wisdom can involve knowing which work should take priority. For example, it is important to plant the field before building your house:

> *Prepare your work outside, get everything ready for you*
> *in the field, and after that build your house.*
> Proverbs 24:27

A modern equivalent might suggest building your financial and career base before taking out a mortgage or a car loan.

Early in my career, I was offered the opportunity to join a small start-up backed by a celebrity chef and a venture fund. The opportunity was intriguing, but once I learned that the founders believed that the executive staff should go first class (company cars, well-furnished offices, etc.) to encourage a "winning" attitude, I decided the job was not for me. I heard later that the company burned through their capital exceptionally quickly; it was sad to hear but I was glad I was not a part of it. My decision was not based on any great wisdom; I think almost anyone with experience in this particular industry would have seen the problem and made the same decision.

How do we develop prudence? Partly through experience, but some other things are also important. We need to be clear about our purpose and long-term objectives, work to discern reality clearly (see the above section on humility), and exercise the self-control required to act in accordance with our goals. I find the last of these to be the most difficult and think this is probably the case with most people. Sometimes we need to pray for the strength to resist temptations and distractions (including clickbait).

An excellent example of prudence is a younger friend who recently graduated from college. While many others had gone into debt to pay for the college of their choice, he resisted the temptation and adamantly refused to borrow money. This meant going to a cheaper college for most of his classes before moving to a university with more specialized offerings in his field. It also meant taking a couple of years longer to obtain the degree he sought. But he emerged debt-free and better prepared to pursue his long-term goals.

Prudence can sound like a boring, penny-pinching kind of virtue. But in some ways it is at the center of a decision process that can lay the foundation for exciting opportunities.

Resilience

Resilience can be an essential quality when we face adversity. It can determine whether or not we bounce back from significant setbacks. Progress and innovation often depend on resilience in the face of rejection.

Resilience is closely related to courage. Many of the factors that help us develop courage apply to resilience as well—things like our sense of purpose, doing the right thing, confidence, a supportive social network, and spiritual practices.

Adaptability and an ability to change course as needed are also important.

The issue of resilience has been with us for a long time. There are many remarkable resilience stories in the Bible, some of which go back to a mostly preliterate society several thousand years ago. Think of Joseph thrown into prison for years and David living in the wilderness, hunted by his enemies.

The Apostle Paul provides a particularly compelling example of resilience. Paul was driven by a powerful sense of mission to reach Gentiles (non-Jews) with his message. This is how he described some of the obstacles he had faced:

> *Five times I have received the forty lashes minus one.*
> *Three times I was beaten with rods. Once I received a*
> *stoning. Three times I was shipwrecked; for a night and a*
> *day I was adrift at sea; on frequent journeys, in danger*
> *from rivers, danger from bandits, danger from my own*
> *people, danger from Gentiles, danger in the city, danger in*
> *the wilderness, danger at sea, danger from false brothers*
> *and sisters; in toil and hardship, through many a sleepless*

*night, hungry and thirsty, often without food, cold and
naked. And, besides other things, I am under daily pressure
because of my anxiety for all the churches.*
2 Corinthians 11:24-28

Paul had a powerful belief that he was being called by God to spread the message of Jesus to the Gentiles. He was absolutely convinced of the truth of this mission and the importance of the role he was called to play. To fulfill this calling, he had to generate an extraordinary level of resilience.

Professor of management Fred Luthans views resilience as "the capacity to rebound or bounce back from adversity, conflict, failure, or even positive events, progress and increased responsibility." He considers it a key psychological resource in the workplace and one that can be developed or strengthened.[48]

Different people seem to have different levels of resilience in different types of situations. One individual might face a particular type of adversity with admirable resilience but then fall apart when faced with another type. For example, think of the person who meets the threat of financial hardship calmly but is cowed by their abusive boss. Maybe such a person has successfully overcome financial hardship in the past but has a high need for approval from authority figures.

Perhaps this has to do with the nature of our confidence and our other strengths. We can have confidence in some of our strengths but not in others, so our resilience is dependent on the specific challenges we face and how they match up with our understanding of our corresponding strengths. If we have a better understanding of our strengths, we might have a better understanding of our resilience.

A sense of coherence and meaning is important. Having a coherent framework through which we view our life, work, and adversity seems to help us deal with stress and maintain our resilience.

Paul had this sense of coherence. He had a framework that put adversity into its proper perspective against a higher, grander reality. He was absolutely convinced that he was doing the work to which God called him, and that if he persisted, his mission would have a lasting impact. This made it easier to deal with the extreme forms of adversity he faced.

It is crucial to develop our own larger perspective as we go through life. Biblical scripture, which developed over thousands of years of adversity, can be an important resource, as can our prayer, study, and reflection.

The content of our faith is critical. If we believe at a deep level in a benevolent God who is on our side, then it is natural to believe that things will ultimately turn out to be okay. If, on the other hand, we believe in an angry, judgmental God, or perhaps one who is aloof, then coherence, optimism, and resilience will be harder to maintain. The Christian message of a loving, grace-giving God can be of enormous help to people facing challenges that require resilience.

Hope

Hope is an essential contributor to our health and sense of well-being and is important for our work effectiveness. It also has a spiritual aspect and is often rooted in our faith. While our faith or spirituality can play an essential role, let's first examine the nature of hope and its close cousin, optimism.

Hope and Optimism

We often use hope and optimism as synonyms; both involve a positive attitude and an expectation of favorable outcomes. Both justify and encourage moving forward despite setbacks and, in most situations, are more likely to lead to better health and positive results than do negative attitudes.

There are differences, however. I think of optimism as more of a disposition, representing a general expectation that things overall will work out. Hope, on the other hand, is usually thought of as more specific and involves a reasonable expectation of a particular positive outcome, such as "I hope to get the new job." The expectation is plausible even though the outcome is not inevitable.

Hope can be either active or passive. It can involve a positive outcome toward which we are working, or it can involve something beyond our control for which we are waiting. Here we focus on active hope, which I believe is the most important to cultivate in the workplace.

A high level of active hope is important for innovation and entrepreneurship and is more likely to move us forward toward a better future.

Active Hope

Psychologist C. R. Snyder provided a valuable framework for what I am calling active hope. He interviewed high-hope individuals and found that hope generally consists of three components: a goal (a desired future outcome), a belief that one has a realistic pathway to this outcome, and the will to follow this pathway. In other words, Snyder went beyond the expectation of a specific favorable outcome and added willpower and an identified path (waypower) to get to the desired outcome.[49]

Snyder presented an important insight: hope is more effective if we identify a path to the desired outcome and actively follow it. Snyder's framework helps us move past debilitating passivity and connect hope with action. It does not guarantee success, but it does make it more likely.

Some people are naturally more positive and hopeful. Genetics might have something to do with this, as can previous positive experiences that have reinforced one's expectation of positive outcomes. But there are things the rest of us can do to develop more.

An obvious first step is to appreciate the positive outcomes we have experienced in the past and notice the ones occurring in the near present. Let's not let them get away without reminding ourselves that positive outcomes do occur.

Snyder's former students and collaborators, Jennifer Cheavens and David Feldman, have used his framework for what they call "hope-therapy." Cheavens and Feldman have found that even people not initially considered to be high-hope individuals can learn to set clear and often challenging goals and sub-goals, develop multiple pathways to reach these goals, anticipate and devise solutions for obstacles they encounter, and work towards them.[50]

Hope In the Bible

At first glance, much of the hope in the Bible seems to be passive hope—people waiting for God to fix things for them.

In our English versions of the Bible, hope most often seems to refer to trusting in God and often involves waiting for God to do something. This waiting and trusting often seem to carry a connotation of passivity that we do not see in Snyder's framework.

But this is not the whole story. If we look at the actual stories of the Bible, we see they are often full of active hope of a type that would fit Snyder's framework. There are many examples of Biblical characters who, often after being informed and inspired by God, pursue desired outcomes by following a clear path and exhibiting considerable willpower, courage, and persistence as they do so. For example:

- Early on, Abraham hears a call to a better life and a message that God will bless all peoples through him and his descendants (Genesis 12:1-3). He and his people set off on a perilous journey through an unknown land, following the direction given by God.
- Joseph anticipates famine in Egypt and goes to work building grain inventories during the fat years with the hope that the people will have food to eat during the famine years.
- Moses returns to Egypt to confront Pharoah and lead his people on a forty-year pilgrimage to the hoped-for Promised Land.
- Nehemiah leaves his comfortable life in Persia to return to Jerusalem to lead the work of rebuilding the city and Temple.
- Esther takes the deliberate and highly dangerous path of lobbying the king to prevent the murder of countless Jews.
- Paul pursues the goal of reaching the Gentiles with the message of Jesus by following a path that takes him across the Mediterranean; in the process, he demonstrates extraordinary willpower.

There are many other examples throughout the Bible, most notably the mission of Jesus. In these examples, hope provides the basis for action; the hero in each story believed that God was with them, but they still acted with agency and willpower and were not sitting back and waiting for God to fix things for them. With God's help, they identified a pathway to the desired end and demonstrated the will and persistence to follow the path. We can do likewise, and our world will be better as a result.

Spirituality and Active Hope Today

I certainly accept the idea that developing the skills identified by Snyder, Cheavens, and Feldman is important for becoming more actively hopeful.

But I also think there might be a spiritual aspect as well. There seem to be times when we feel empowered or inspired by something that is deeper than or beyond our normal experience. Some Christians might say that God or his Holy Spirit is working in or through us, but however we think of it, this mysterious feeling of inspiration can be a profound source of hope, especially if it can be channeled through the framework proposed by Snyder.

Theological grounding can help cultivate this feeling. Theology by its nature turns our attention toward the mystery of God and transcendent reality and helps us develop a sense of coherence that is essential for hope in the face of setbacks. Theology can also help us reflect on our purpose and values and think seriously about the desired outcomes to which we are willing to commit ourselves. It can inspire by reminding us of the bigger picture.

We can also study biblical exemplars like those mentioned above and reflect on how they faced their challenges, and what the lessons might be for how we face our challenges.

Most important, at least to my way of thinking, are spiritual practices like prayer, meditation, worship, and reflection. These help us turn our attention toward God and the divine mystery. They can be a source of strength and wisdom and help us move forward with a deeper sense of purpose.

In the Bible, it often seems that the people who are most effective at reaching their goal are the ones who feel empowered by God. In contemporary terms, we might think of this as having a deep, intuitive sense that we are moving in the right direction; for some, this might involve a feeling that they are aligned with a greater purpose.

We are more likely to have a powerful sense of hope in our work lives if we feel this sense of spiritual connection. We are more likely to know where we are going and how we plan to get there, and more likely to have the will and persistence to see it through. And we are more likely to feel empowered and perhaps affirmed as we move into the future and face new challenges and uncertainties with courage and hope.

Chapter Six

Spiritual Practices for Your Workday

At the beginning of this book, I wrote of the deep, intuitive desire many of us have to connect with something deeper than ourselves—to experience a deeper sense of connection with God. Prayer and related practices are an important aspect of this for many people.

These practices also have practical benefits. They can help us calm down, be more alert, and act with strength and wisdom as we face challenges and opportunities. They also help us develop a deeper sense of mission and purpose.

Our focus in this chapter will be on practices that involve prayer, especially ones that can be integrated into the rhythm of our work lives.

Prayer is not the only way people feel connected with the sacred; there are many other modes, depending on the person involved. People can experience the sacred through music, worship, scripture, nature, community, and various physical activities. If we believe that all of life is in some mysterious way grounded in God, then it is logical for us to expect to experience the sacred in activities that are not overtly religious. We should pray, but it is also good to identify other modes that evoke in us a sense of the sacred and then deliberately set aside time to participate in them.

Thoughts on Prayer

Different people speak of prayer in different ways and have different expectations and apparently different types of experiences. Some people speak of prayer as a sort of conversation with God. For others, it is more of a petition in which they speak of their hopes and fears. For some, it is a chance to become quiet in a special place and reconnect with what is most real for them.

I think of prayer as opening ourselves to a possible reality beyond what we can see and touch, perhaps something beyond what we usually think of as ordinary reality. We hope to open ourselves to God and maybe experience something like a subtle spiritual prompting, an intuition, an insight, or maybe a sense of peace or calm in the face of turmoil.

Entering the Sacred Silence

The more profound prayer experiences are likely to involve silence of some sort; I think of this as sacred silence. This can involve the external or objective silence associated with a quiet environment—a quiet room, a silent retreat, an empty church, or perhaps a period of silence during a religious activity of some sort.

As one of the psalms puts it:

> *Be still, and know that I am God!*
> *Psalm 46:10*

But it can also be an internal silence experienced despite being in a noisy external setting. For example, someone might experience a bit of contemplative silence while listening to music or a sermon, watching children play, or even while going through a crisis. To some extent, when we speak of silence, we are speaking of an internal state, not necessarily the absence of external noise, though a quiet setting can undoubtedly be helpful. The silence we are discussing involves a sense of the sacred— perhaps of connection with a reality beyond the world of ordinary experience.

We might occasionally experience a sense of awe, either as we pray or as a stimulus to prayer. Awe can be defined as experiencing something of the infinite vastness of reality, a vastness beyond our comprehension. The experience of awe can be exciting and enlivening, even in the small doses we are most likely to encounter.

The sacred silence can lead us into a deeper prayer or meditative state. Practices designed to facilitate this are sometimes referred to as contemplative practices. With these practices,we use one or more techniques to quiet and focus our mind as we turn our attention to God. As we do so, we allow ourselves to drift into a deeper state of prayer.

Of the practices described below, the breath prayer, *Lectio Divina*, and the visualization exercise are often considered contemplative. In some cases, the shorter practices could also be contemplative; this depends on the circumstances and the predisposition of the person.

Sacred silence is not the only way to describe these experiences. People also speak of experiencing the presence of God, feeling a sense of transcendence, connecting with something deeper than themselves, becoming centered and grounded, and becoming conscious of a greater reality. Prayer experiences are often hard to define and describe, so it is reasonable that people use a variety of different words when talking about them.

Prayer in the Bible

There are many examples of prayer in the Bible. Some sound like conversations, others like petitions. Some involve a feeling of extraordinary awe.

Here we will explore three examples of prayer in the New Testament, each involving Jesus, and each with a particular insight for our work lives. As always, be alert to how each passage might connect with your own experience and what it might be saying to you.

The Lord's Prayer - Matthew 6:7-13

The Lord's Prayer is the best-known prayer in the Bible and is frequently memorized and included in church services. It is based on a passage from Matthew's account of the Sermon on the Mount, though the language is a little different in Matthew than that recited in most churches. Matthew quotes Jesus as follows:

> *When you are praying, do not heap up empty phrases*
> *as the Gentiles do; for they think that they will be heard*
> *because of their many words. Do not be like them, for*
> *your Father knows what you need before you ask him.*

> *Pray then in this way:*
> *Our Father in heaven,*
> *hallowed be your name.*
> *Your kingdom come.*
> *Your will be done,*
> *on earth as it is in heaven.*
> *Give us this day our daily bread.*
> *And forgive us our debts,*
> *as we also have forgiven our debtors.*
> *And do not bring us to the time of trial,*
> *but rescue us from the evil one.*
>   *Matthew 6:7-13*

At first glance, this appears to be a prayer of supplication—it is asking for something. But note what the prayer requests: for the most part, the person praying asks for a change in attitude. Note also the specifics: that we treat God as holy; that his kingdom comes (i.e., help us be loyal to God and to participate in his kingdom); that God's will be done; that we forgive others (as we are forgiven); and that we not be confronted with temptation. With the possible exception of daily bread, the prayer seems to focus our attention on our relationship with God and with other people.

Sixteenth-century reformer Martin Luther believed that daily bread referred to everything we need for a healthy, flourishing life consistent with the biblical concept of shalom:

> Daily bread includes everything needed for this life, such as food, drink, clothing, shoes, house, home, fields, cattle, money, goods, God-fearing spouse and children, faithful servants and rulers, good government, good weather, peace, health, order, honor, true friends, good neighbors, and the like.[51]

Luther believed that this part of the prayer was intended to acknowledge God's provision and lead us into an attitude of thanksgiving.

If you prayed this prayer every day, how do you think it would change your work attitude? I think it might help us be more mindful of God, more spiritually open, more forgiving of our coworkers, and more alert to the dangers of temptation.

Prayer and Mission - Mark 1:35-39

Most of us would like to work with a deeper, more definite, more robust sense of mission. A story from Mark 1:35-39 can provide some insight into how prayer might help. I think you will find that this passage has something important to say about the the possible relationship between prayer and our work and in particular between prayer and the sense of mission we bring to our work.

The story takes place early in the ministry of Jesus, while he was still in the region of Galilee. Picture the setting: Jesus had been attracting followers and building his ministry in a town called Capernaum. For some reason (we are not told why), Jesus got up while it was still dark and went off to pray by himself:

> *In the morning, while it was still very dark, Jesus got*
> *up and went out to a deserted place and there he prayed.*
> *And Simon and his companions hunted for him. When*
> *they found Jesus they said to him, "Everyone is searching*
> *for you." Jesus answered, "Let us go on to the neighboring*
> *towns so that I may proclaim the message there also; for*
> *that is what I came out to do."*
> *And he went throughout Galilee proclaiming the*
> *message in their synagogues and casting out demons.*
> *Mark 1:35-39*

It appears that in the process of turning toward God at night in the dark, Jesus developed a renewed or perhaps a clarified sense of mission. Perhaps he received a new insight or new inspiration. Or maybe the experience strengthened his resolve in some way.

In the meantime, back in the village, the disciples woke up and saw that Jesus was not there, so they went looking for him. When they found him, they probably expected Jesus to return to Capernaum to continue his very successful ministry there. That would be the normal thing to do—what most of us would do—keep doing what we find is successful and build on that success.

But instead, Jesus announced that he was going to the other towns and villages throughout the region to proclaim his message to a broader range of people.

I believe that this decision led to a greatly expanded ministry with, as we know now, a much more significant impact. Was there a connection between this critical decision and his prayer experience? I am convinced that there was.

Mark does not tell us how Jesus prayed in this particular case, but I would imagine that it was probably silent or listening prayer, what we could call receptive prayer. With receptive prayer, we might begin by expressing whatever is on our mind, maybe a concern or question. But then we become quiet and receptive, and that is the point.

One way to do this is to find a quiet place and time, sit quietly for a couple of minutes, and then turn your attention toward God and pray. You can begin by expressing whatever is on your mind. And then sit quietly for a few more minutes, prayerfully, receptively.

Keep in mind that it is not the method or the technique that matters but your orientation and attitude. The important thing is to turn your attention toward God and pray in whatever way seems most suitable.

Prayer and Decisiveness - Luke 6:12-19

Luke presents another example of prayer from early in the ministry of Jesus. Here, too, Jesus goes off by himself to pray at night:

> *Now during those days Jesus went out to the mountain to pray; and he spent the night in prayer to God.*
>
> *And when day came, he called his disciples and chose twelve of them, whom he also named apostles: Simon, whom he named Peter, and his brother Andrew, and James, and John, and Philip, and Bartholomew, and Matthew, and Thomas, and James son of Alphaeus,*

and Simon, who was called the Zealot, and Judas son of
James, and Judas Iscariot, who became a traitor.
    He came down with them and stood on a level place,
with a great crowd of his disciples and a great multitude
of people from all Judea, Jerusalem, and the coast of Tyre
and Sidon. They had come to hear him and to be healed
of their diseases; and those who were troubled with
unclean spirits were cured.
    And all in the crowd were trying to touch him, for
power came out from him and healed all of them.
Luke 6:12-19

One can only imagine what it would have been like for Jesus to spend the night on the mountain, praying to God.

Notice how decisively and powerfully he acted in the morning. In apparently quick succession, he appointed the twelve apostles from among his followers and then preached and healed with power.

Did his prayer experience help Jesus to act this effectively? I think it did. There is something about prayer that seems to center us and helps us think clearly and make good decisions. Many of the practices discussed in this chapter are intended to calm us down and make us aware of God and the divine mystery. As we quiet our minds and calm our emotions, we are more likely to make better decisions. And it helps a great deal if we can become more aware of God and our spiritual promptings.

————

Each of these examples of prayer involves turning toward God and each involves some sort of personal transformation. The Lord's Prayer is mostly about our attitude toward God and other people and perhaps about asking for our character to be changed. In Mark 1:35-39, there is a connection between prayer and mission. And in the Luke passage, there seems to be a connection between spending time in prayer and then acting decisively and with power. As applied to our work lives, each story says something meaningful about turning toward God in prayer and its importance. We should pray more.

Weaving Spiritual Practices Into Our Work Lives

The practices most helpful in our daily work will be the ones that help us turn our attention toward God and lead us into a deeper experience of the sacred and, at the same time, can be integrated into our daily work pattern.

Most of us cannot afford to spend several hours a day in prayer; this would obviously not be realistic and would not respect our work and our work-related obligations. A proper regard for both spiritual practices and work requires us to integrate both of these in a way that respects both. We need practices that flow with our work and help us deepen the spiritual connection we experience during the day.

This involves a conundrum. To work productively, we need to be seriously engaged in what we are doing; you might say we need to be fully absorbed in the task. But if we are fully absorbed in our work, then in the moment we have little or no bandwidth available for anything else—including our theology. How, then, can we be mindful of God and our spirituality as we work?

Perhaps we should think of prayer and other spiritual practices as preparing us and setting the context for work, even if we are not thinking about theology as we perform our tasks. This context can include our sense of mission, our values and priorities, and our general understanding of our relationship to God.

———

Most people find it helpful to establish a regular daily pattern for their spiritual practices. But while a pattern of daily practice is best, most of us have trouble maintaining such a schedule until and unless it becomes a habit. An alternative might be to commit to a practice three times a week and then increase the frequency as it begins to feel more natural. Over time we become increasingly aware of the value of the spiritual practice and find it natural to perform it more often.

The Need for Discernment

We should exercise a degree of caution if we believe that, while praying, we have received something like a new insight or sense of being called.

Discernment is essential; there is usually a risk that we are misinterpreting our experience or deluding ourselves as to its source. Christians have traditionally engaged in discernment by testing their experience against scripture and asking for the advice of other Christians, perhaps in a group pulled together for this purpose.

But it is also important to apply common sense. Does the insight seem to make sense from a practical point of view? If not, then perhaps we should be especially careful about acting on it.

Examples of Spiritual Practices

Most of the following practices can be easily done during the workday and should integrate with the rhythms of our work quite well. There are a few exceptions, which I will note.

If you find it difficult to relax enough to perform one of these practices, try preparing for the practice with the breath prayer that follows below. This practice involves simply observing your breath passively as you inhale and exhale. It has been used for many centuries to quiet the mind, calm the emotions, and prepare us to be more receptive.

There are a few other things to keep in mind as you experiment with the practices.

Spiritual experience is not automatic; whether or not we experience something sacred is beyond our control. We can enter the silence and pay attention, but we cannot force or control the experience. There is no magic formula that says first we do this and then something specific happens.

The main thing is to turn your attention toward God as fully as you can; this applies whether the practice is short or long. Various techniques have been developed over the centuries and by various religions to help us do this more deeply, but the important thing is not the technique but your orientation.

Remember that while these practices can help you work better, that is not the main purpose. The main purpose is to turn our attention toward God during the workday. We want to express something of the sacred in our work, not try to harness the sacred in some way. We should think of the spirit of God as wild and untamable, not as something we can bend to our will.

We are each wired differently and come to both our work and our spiritual practices with our own predispositions and circumstances. Moreover, these factors change by day and maybe by hour; therefore, it is essential to have a range of spiritual practices from which to draw. Most of us will find some practices more useful than others and will probably tend to go back to a favorite practice or two, but we can still benefit from having several options available. I suggest you experiment with these practices and choose the ones that you find most helpful.

We begin with the shorter practices.

Breath Prayer

A breath exercise, or breath prayer, is very simple but effective for calming us and helping us focus. It can be used by itself or in combination with one of the other practices in this chapter. It has often been used for secular meditation but can also be used to usher us into a prayerful state.

Here is one way to do it. Sit straight but comfortably in a quiet place, with your eyes closed. Say a short prayer of gratitude, and then take one comfortably deep breath, gently letting it in and out. As you do so, observe the sensation of the air coming in and then flowing out. Breathe normally after taking the first breath, continuing to observe your breath and the associated sensations. Except for the first breath, the point is not to change your breathing, but to observe it as a way to relax and refocus. As you become more relaxed, turn your attention toward God and pray silently.

If your mind wanders, gently turn your attention back toward your breath without fighting the unwanted thoughts—just let them drift away on their own. If you focus your attention on one thing—such as your breath—your unrelated mental activity will eventually begin to quiet down and your unwanted thoughts will tend to drift away, as long as you do not give them any energy by fighting them.

You can try other variations. For example, you could say a silent prayer of thanksgiving with each breath. Or you could incorporate a prayer mantra or the Jesus Prayer, as described below.

Sometimes it helps to set a timer so that you will not be preoccupied with how much time the exercise is taking. When the timer goes off, the exercise is over and it is time to engage the task at hand with new energy and concentration. Doing this exercise for a short period is unlikely to lead to a deep meditative state, but it should have a noticeably calming and focusing effect and might prove to be energizing as you return to work.

Sanctifying the Workplace

Denise Daniels and Shannon Vandewarker, in their book *Working in the Presence of God: Spiritual Practices of Ordinary Work*, suggest walking through your workplace before you start the day, praying for the people and the events that will take place.[52] Doing so is bound to affect our attitude toward our coworkers and our work.

You can also reinforce the sense of the sacred at other times during the day. While it might feel awkward or inappropriate to pray loudly in a secular workplace, you can still visit the various places where you will be working and pray silently.

Prayer Brackets

I spoke earlier of the paradox of wanting to experience a spiritual connection as we work, but also needing to concentrate fully on the work-related task at hand. If we are to perform the task well, we need to be fully engaged; this does not leave room for simultaneous theologizing.

One possible solution is to bracket our tasks with prayer; I sometimes call this using prayer brackets.

With prayer brackets, you offer a brief prayer before and after the task. The first prayer asks God to help you focus on the job at hand and do the work well. Then you focus on the task. After the work, you thank God for the opportunity to focus on the task and to do good work.

The point is to surround the task with prayer without interrupting it. You might say your faith or spirituality provides the context or framework for the task without diverting your attention from it. You work with full intensity on the task, but still cultivate your overall sense of spiritual connection and purpose.

Caleb Monroe, a leader of the faith and work movement in Los Angeles and a member of the staff at Reality Church of Los Angeles, has developed an interesting example. He suggests offering something like the following prayer before we begin a task; Monroe is also a professional writer and uses this himself.

> Because this work demands my full attention, I make
> my attention an offering: please accept it as my contin-
> uous prayer. Grant me the grace to remain in your
> presence as I write, prosper me with your assistance,
> receive all my work, and possess all my affections.
> Amen.

Monroe has written that "the first sentence is inspired by the Simone Weil quote 'attention, taken to its highest degree, is the same thing as prayer,' and the second sentence is adapted from a prayer of Brother Lawrence, recorded by Joseph de Beaufort in his introduction to the *Practice of the Presence of God.*"

After this first prayer, perform the task while giving it your full attention. Then, after completing the task, offer a prayer of gratitude.

Prayer as Preparation for Meetings and Difficult Conversations

If you find yourself becoming annoyed or disengaged in a meeting, remind yourself that everyone in the meeting has dignity and special value; we might say that each person has been created in the image of God. This has implications for how we work with them.

A friend told me a story from his own work life that illustrates this:

> Dave (a pseudonym) found himself dreading his
> weekly financial meetings. These were not pleasant
> events, especially since the business was not doing well
> and there was a lot of finger pointing and an undercur-
> rent of blame and annoyance. One day he prayed by
> himself before one of these dreaded meetings. He asked
> God to work through him and to remind him that each
> person in the meeting was made in the image of God
> and should be treated accordingly.

This prayer, which he repeated over the following weeks, had a remarkable effect on his attitude and helped him engage the people in the meeting in a much more positive manner. Over time, this began to influence the attitude of the other participants as well. While the situation did not become miraculously perfect, the meetings did improve and the participants became more engaged, positive, and cooperative. Dave no longer dreaded the meetings.

Saying a brief, silent prayer, and remembering that the other participants have inherent value in God's eyes, can do wonders for our working relationships, especially if done before a meeting or difficult conversation.

The Lord's Prayer

Jesus's recommendation for prayer is included in the passage referred to earlier from Matthew 6:5-15. Most churches use slightly different wording than Matthew; the meaning is very similar, but it is a little easier to recite. Here is one version:

> *Our Father who art in heaven,*
> *hallowed be thy name.*
> *Thy kingdom come.*
> *Thy will be done,*
> *on earth as it is in heaven.*
> *Give us this day our daily bread.*
> *And forgive us our debts,*
> *as we forgive our debtors.*
> *And lead us not into temptation,*
> *but deliver us from evil.*
> *For thine is the kingdom and the power and the glory*
> *forever.*
> *Amen.*

The Prayer Mantra

Over the years, I have found one of the most useful spiritual practices is one I call the prayer mantra. This practice has been especially beneficial when dealing with stress, whether the stressful issue has been a minor hassle or a crisis large enough to keep me awake at night. There is something about the right mantra that puts the current crisis into a proper perspective, connects us to a deeper reality, and helps us refocus and act with greater effectiveness.

For our purposes, we can define a mantra as a short phrase or series of words used in prayer, meditation, or other spiritual practice. The term is sometimes used more generally in secular settings as a phrase that reminds one of an oft-repeated principle or goal (e.g., "our mantra is that the customer always comes first"), but in this discussion, I limit the use of the term to its more spiritual sense.

A mantra is often repeated continuously in order to lead one into a meditative state. A prayer mantra can be used in this way as well, but it can also be repeated once or twice as a quick prayer; this is how I use it.

The mantra that has been most effective for me is, "Thy will be done." I think its power arises from how it turns my attention toward God and reminds me of eternity and a higher, more powerful reality. The rhythm or cadence of the syllables also seems to contribute to its calming and refocusing effect. You might try this yourself; close your eyes, turn your attention toward God, and repeat "thy will be done" once or multiple times. Or choose your own phrase.

———

People sometimes think of mantras as Hindu or Vedic, and in fact, the word itself originates in Sanskrit, a language of ancient India. But most of the major religious traditions, including Christianity, have their own equivalents of mantras.

In some religious cultures, the sound of an adopted mantra is essential. Rhythm, alliteration, and rhyme can all contribute to the effect. For some, the effect is created exclusively by the sound, not the meaning of the words. This sound can have a magical connotation in the mind of some people, with the sound itself believed to affect the spiritual world (this idea is the origin of pseudo-magical incantations such as hocus-pocus and abraca-dabra). But in other cases, the sound itself is seen not so much as magical but as having a psychological effect on the hearer. Some eastern spiritual teachers even recommend mantras in a language that the meditator does not understand so that the meditator hears the sound but does not become distracted by the meaning of the words.

In the West, and particularly within Christianity, the meaning and devotional aspect of the words take precedence. The sound can contribute, but the meaning of the words is the primary factor. Within the Christian tradition, mantras are directed toward God as a form of prayer.

Some people use the words of the Jesus Prayer (see below) as a mantra; it is a little longer than most others. One could also use a short, memorized passage of scripture, or any other phrase that has meaning to the individual (e.g., "praise God," "thank you, Jesus"). It helps to have a mantra that has been used frequently and has become a habit.

Whether or not you are going through a time of stress at this moment, I recommend that you take a few minutes and select a mantra for your own use. A favorite passage or expression might suggest some possibilities.

The Jesus Prayer

The Jesus Prayer was developed within the Eastern Orthodox tradition at least 1,200 years ago. It can be found in the *Philokalia*,[53] a collection of Eastern Orthodox theological reflections and mystical writings. This prayer can be used as a mantra during times of stress as well as during calmer times.

A common version of the prayer is:

Lord Jesus, Son of God, have mercy on me, a sinner.

The Jesus Prayer is often synchronized with one's breath and can be combined with the breath prayer described above. Repetition and attention to breath tend to move one toward a meditative state, while the words themselves turn our attention toward God.

John Cassian's Prayer

John Cassian (360-435 CE) recommended a repetitive prayer based on Psalm 40:

> O God, make speed to save me: O Lord, make haste to help me.[54]

He used this prayer to resist temptation and other distractions. It too can calm us down and help us focus our attention.

Physical Prayer

Some people find it useful to pray with their bodies. One can, for example, lift one's eyes and arms to the sky as one prays. Or one can sit with head bowed and palms face up and open. Sometimes the physicality of these types of prayer can represent a refreshing break from our work.

The position and motion of our bodies can affect our attitude, including our attitude as we pray.

Standing Prayer

I have been told that in at least a few cases, early monks used a form of standing prayer while they were working. If a monk felt tired or bored or otherwise felt a need for prayer, he was to stand up at his workstation, say a quick prayer (which for our purposes might be silent), and then sit down and go back to work.[55]

This prayer provided a distinct physical break which enabled the monk to more easily turn his attention toward God while also making it easy to get back to work quickly. The act of standing up, saying a quick prayer, and sitting back down can play the same role for us as it did for the monks.

Walking Prayer

Another form of physical prayer is what some people call walking prayer; I find this useful when I have been sitting at a desk for too long. Go for a walk! And as you do so, turn your attention toward God and thank him for what you see (but watch out for traffic). You can repeat a prayer or prayer mantra, or you can acknowledge your surroundings with gratitude. And, of course, ear buds offer all kinds of opportunities for recorded reflections, Bible readings, and music.

Symbols and Icons

For some people, a visual reminder such as an icon, image, or sacred object can help them enter a more spiritual or sacred frame of mind. Images are usually processed more quickly and intuitively than words. This can also apply to objects that are held in the hand.

The Eastern Orthodox Church has made extensive use of icons. These follow distinctive patterns and are regarded by some as a window through which one can experience a feeling of transcendence. The point is not to interpret the image but rather to gaze at it contemplatively and to allow it to move us spiritually; sometimes this involves a feeling that we are entering or going through the picture. Other objects (crosses, figurines) can help remind us who we are and keep us grounded, especially if they have particular significance for us.

A sacred object is one in which we see some sort of connection with the divine because of either our interpretation of its meaning or our previous experience with it. Sacred objects can be kept in our work area within view as a reminder. Or they can be kept in a drawer to be brought out as needed, hidden away during normal times so that they do not become commonplace and lose their sense of sacredness.

Post-It Note Prayer

We sometimes have worries that will not go away and about which we are not in a position to take action. One technique that some have found useful is to identify whatever it is that they are worried about and then write it down on a Post-it note or other small piece of paper. They then prayerfully offer it to God with the idea of leaving it to him, and as they do so, they crumple up the note or paper and throw it in the trash.

There is something about the physical action of writing down the worry, looking at it, and then crumpling and throwing it away that seems to make the act of letting it go seem more concrete. Of course, this is only appropriate for problems and regrets about which we can do nothing, not for problems that we should engage and try to solve.

Prayers of Praise and Gratitude

Prayers of praise are closely related to prayers of gratitude, and we know that gratitude makes an important contribution to our subjective well-being.

Prayers of praise often express our gratitude to God. I have attended small group meetings that began with a prayer of praise. In each case, the group was led into a prayerful silence and then, after a minute or two, participants spontaneously offered expressions of praise and gratitude to God, both specific and general. I found it very moving.

You might also spend a few minutes before work each day in prayer and, in the process, thank God for three things for which you are grateful. This is bound to increase your gratitude toward God and improve your attitude as you begin the workday.[56]

One could also recite a psalm of praise and gratitude. One example would be Psalm 100:

> *Make a joyful noise to the LORD, all the earth.*
> *Worship the LORD with gladness;*
> * come into his presence with singing.*
> *Know that the LORD is God.*
> *It is he that made us, and we are his;*
> * we are his people, and the sheep of his pasture.*
> *Enter his gates with thanksgiving,*
> * and his courts with praise.*
> *Give thanks to him, bless his name.*
> *For the LORD is good;*
> * his steadfast love endures forever,*
> *and his faithfulness to all generations.*
> *Psalm 100*

Prayer can express gratitude for particular people or aspects of our lives; it can also acknowledge the greatness, sovereignty, or transcendence of God.

Prayers of Lament

Things can go painfully wrong at work and in our lives. Some of us might not think of complaining to God, but the Bible is full of cases where this happens; prayers of lament are quite acceptable from the point of view of Christian theology. By expressing our complaints to God in prayer, we are better able to bring our whole selves into the prayer.

Express your complaint to God as fully, openly, and authentically as you can. Then ask for help.

In the Bible, Psalms of lament typically begin with the complaint, ask God for help (and often supply a reason why God should help), and then express hope in God's eventual salvation. We can follow the same pattern.

Psalm 13 is an example:

> *How long, O LORD? Will you forget me forever?*
> *How long will you hide your face from me?*
> *How long must I bear pain in my soul,*
>   *and have sorrow in my heart all day long?*
> *How long shall my enemy be exalted over me?*
> *Consider and answer me, O LORD my God!*
> *Give light to my eyes, or I will sleep the sleep of death,*
>   *and my enemy will say, "I have prevailed"; my foes will*
>   *rejoice because I am shaken.*
> *But I trusted in your steadfast love;*
>   *my heart shall rejoice in your salvation.*
> *I will sing to the LORD,*
>   *because he has dealt bountifully with me.*
> *Psalm 13*

Reading Scripture as Prayer

Incorporating scripture in prayer and other spiritual practices can add richness to our experience; scripture can speak to us at a deep level. Biblical scripture plays a key role in many spiritual practices, and reading and reflecting on scripture is probably the second most frequent Christian spiritual practice, after prayer.

The Bible developed over several thousand years as people grappled with the deep questions of God and human existence. It emerged from the legitimate spiritual experiences and subsequent reflection of people who went before us. Because it often originated in profound spiritual experiences, the Bible might stimulate our own spiritual experience if we read it with a degree of spiritual receptivity. This is especially true if we read the great biblical narratives while we are in a prayerful, meditative state.

The Bible was written in much different cultures than those of today and therefore can shift our thinking and encourage new perspectives. Much of the Bible grew out of times of extreme crisis and therefore might have special meaning for a reader facing a crisis today.

The practices in this section tend to be somewhat longer. They also lend themselves to a deeper, more contemplative experience.

Beginning the practice with the breath prayer (see pages 114-115) might help you enter a deeper, more meditative state as you read the passage.

Lectio Divina

Lectio Divina, or sacred reading, focuses attention on scripture in a distinctive way. It was originally developed for monks and other members of religious orders but can also make an important contribution to our contemporary work life. It does, however, take more time than most of the other practices in this chapter.

Lectio Divina as a term has been present within the Christian tradition since at least the time of Origen (190 CE), though the meaning has probably varied over time. Origen used the term to refer to a prayerful (perhaps contemplative) reading of scripture with a desire to discern the hidden meaning behind its metaphors. Somewhat later, theologians and church leaders like Ambrose, Augustine, and Benedict, used the term in a similar manner, referring to a prayerful, contemplative reading of scripture in the hope that God would reveal himself in a profound way through the text.

In the twelfth century, a Carthusian monk and prior named Guigo II developed a four-step process that might have established the pattern we know as *Lectio Divina* today. As he put it in his book, *The Ladder for Monks: A Letter on the Contemplative Life:*

> One day when I was busy working with my hands I
> began to think about our spiritual work, and all at once
> four stages in spiritual exercise came into my mind:
> reading, meditation, prayer, and contemplation. These
> make a ladder for monks by which they are lifted from
> earth to heaven.[57]

While it is unclear whether Guigo was thinking in terms of a single exercise, we use something like this four-step process today for *Lectio Divina.*

Lectio Divina begins with prayer, and then a particular passage is read four times, each time preceded and followed by a few minutes of prayerful silence. Here is one way to do it:

- Begin with a brief prayer. You might thank God for the day and ask that you be able to hear what the passage is saying. Then sit quietly with your eyes closed for a couple of minutes as you relax and drift into a deeper prayer state.
- **First Reading:** Read or listen to the passage in its natural or literal sense. If it is a story, what is happening? Then sit in silence for a minute or two.
- **Second Reading:** As you read or listen to the passage again, notice if a word, phrase, or image stands out for you. Then sit silently for a couple of minutes with your attention drawn to this word, phrase, or image.
- **Third Reading:** As you read or listen to the passage again, and in the following silence, listen for any special meaning the passage might have for you. Do you sense a call to be or do something?

Sit quietly in the silence for a couple of minutes, or however long seems right to you.

- **Fourth Reading:** As the passage is read, just sit quietly and let the words wash over you. Don't try to analyze or think about the words—just rest.
- After a few more minutes of silence, say a brief prayer of gratitude and, when you are ready, open your eyes and bring the prayerful state to an end.
- Spend a few minutes thinking about what your experience might mean. If other people have done the exercise with you, talk about your experience.

Including time for prayer, silence, and reflection, this practice can take thirty or so minutes; this can make it difficult for most of us to incorporate it into the workday, but it is worth the time if we can manage to do it.

Previously mentioned authors Daniels and Vandewarker recommend a version that is shorter and involves three rather than four readings.[58] In the first step, we slowly read or listen to the passage, paying attention to the words. The second time, we listen for a word or phrase that seems to stand out (do not try to predict what this will be—it might surprise you). In the third reading, we pay attention to what the word or phrase might be saying to us about our workday; we then take it with us throughout the day.

The practice should begin and end in prayer and there should be several minutes of prayerful silence between each reading. As with the other practices, the important thing is not the time spent but the fullness of attention given to it.

Passage Visualization

Another way to enhance our engagement with scripture is to use a visualization technique. The fourteenth-century Carthusian monk Ludolph of Saxony developed, or at least popularized, such a practice. Ignatius of Loyola, the founder of the Jesuits, picked up and borrowed Ludolph's method for his *Spiritual Exercises*; this practice is sometimes referred to as Ignatian meditation.

A distinctive aspect of this practice is how it ignites the imagination. Participants frequently express surprise at how vividly they experience particular passages of scripture, sometimes to the point of feeling that they are actually within the story being narrated.

For this practice, one uses a passage with a narrative with a single setting that can be imagined. Because of the possibly deeper engagement in the story, it is crucial to choose a passage with positive value for the participant. Do not use passages dealing with judgment, punishment, sin, suffering, pain, etc.

One normally listens to another person read the passage out loud. If you are doing it by yourself, then pick a passage that you know well or is at least short enough that it can be remembered without being read during the exercise. You do not have to remember the story exactly as long as you remember the details that seem most important to you.

Begin by saying a brief prayer and then sitting in silence for a couple minutes. Then imagine what it would be like to be in the setting. In your imagination, what do you see? Hear? Feel? Smell? One then reads or listens to or remembers the story and imagines being in it.

If you are looking for passages to engage in this manner, I often go to the first chapter of the Gospel According to Mark. Mark 1:9-11 and Mark 1:16-20 might be particularly good choices.

Daily Devotions

You might already have a practice of daily devotions, or maybe you have had one in the past. In any case, here are some thoughts you might find useful. Daily devotions based on prayer and the reading of scripture can be particularly meaningful but require setting aside time each day. Most people prefer the early morning hours for this exercise, perhaps during your first cup of coffee or tea, but pick whatever time is best for you.

Daily devotions can be especially helpful for preparing us for the workday. These devotions do not have to be complicated and are easy to design for yourself. This is a time of intentionally turning toward God before entering the busy workday; it can ground us in a deeper sense of meaning that we hope will guide and inspire us.

A common pattern would be to begin with a prayer, followed by the reading of a passage of scripture. You can then reflect on what the passage might be saying to you and how this applies to your work life. The devotion could end with a prayer of gratitude and preparation. As you go through the workday, try to keep the passage and your reflections in mind.

For scripture, my personal preference is usually for a narrative passage, such as a story, but yours might be different. The passage can be selected in various ways; you can choose one at random or select a book of the Bible to read in stages over several days. For narratives, I most frequently turn to the four gospels (Matthew, Mark, Luke, and John), Genesis, and the Acts of the Apostles. If you prefer nonnarrative material that speaks to theological issues, then you might read the Psalms, Isaiah, or the New Testament letters.

On the other hand, if you would prefer to follow a Bible study guide, there are a great many that can be used for this purpose; most are designed for weekly small group meetings, but there is no reason why they could not be used by individuals for daily devotions.

If you decide to use a guide, my advice would be to keep it simple. Most guides have more material than you need for a devotional. The point is to turn our attention toward God and perhaps glean some insights from scripture that you can apply to your work. There are many ways to do this and there is no need for it to be complicated.

Reflecting Upon Our Work - The Prayer of Examen

We are often too busy during the day to seriously reflect on our work's spiritual dimension. It can therefore be quite helpful to take time at the end of the day to review and reflect on our experience and its spiritual significance. A traditional practice known as the Examen can help.

The Examen is a tool for examining one's thoughts and actions from a spiritual perspective. It helps us correct our shortcomings, strengthen our virtues, and, in general, deepen our sense of awareness of God. We do this by examining our thoughts, actions, and feelings over the period involved, usually the just completed day, in considerable detail. As we do so, examine our state of mind at the various times and how it changed as we went through the day.

Ignatius of Loyola, who promoted the Examen in the sixteenth century, thought of it as discerning the movement of good and evil spirits within us. Today we might think of it as examining our spiritual and psychological disposition as we went through the activities of the day. In either case, the Examen can help us be more alert to the spiritual aspects of our lives.

Ignatius advocated two types of Examen—the General and the Particular. In the General Examen, all thoughts, feelings, and actions are subject to review and correction as necessary. The Particular Examen is somewhat similar, but the practitioner focuses on one particular type of sin, notes each occurrence during the day, and resolves to do better.

With either type, we enter into a quiet frame of mind and, in prayer, ask God to help us look back over the day or other period and review our spiritual orientation. We think back to what we were doing and thinking at the beginning of the period and notice our spiritual and psychological condition. We then let our memory take us forward through the rest of the period as we notice the changes in this condition. When did we seem to be moving with God? When did we seem to be moving away? Were our emotions negative or positive? What was our attitude toward the people with whom we were working?

We can often see our work's spiritual significance better in retrospect than when we are in the midst of it.

An abbreviated version of this exercise that focuses on a shorter time frame can also be quite helpful. You might pause after performing a task or having a meeting with one of your coworkers and, after saying a brief prayer, try to examine what you were experiencing during the activity, psychologically and spiritually. This practice does not have to be time-consuming and the fact that we can perform it right after the event in question means that our recollections will be fresh.

We will become more naturally aware of our spirituality as we go through the workday if we can make the Examen a habit.

The Sabbath

Most of us know that it can be quite beneficial to periodically take time off from work and our responsibilities. The Sabbath can be a great gift for us. It can be a day of rest and refreshment, a day when we can recharge and replenish, a day that might even lead us into the rhythm of a richer, fuller life and a greater awareness of the sacred. But many of us, myself included, are not necessarily good at this.

The Bible has many references to the Sabbath. In the first creation story in the book of Genesis, God works for six days and then rests on the seventh day. This becomes the basis for the Sabbath as a day of rest each week (Genesis 2:2-3).

The Sabbath began as a gift, but over time it seemed to have become a collection of rules specifying in detail what we can and cannot do on that day. Rather than a time of rest, it seemed to become an obligation designed to show religious obedience. In some settings, the penalty for violating the Sabbath could even be death by stoning (Numbers 15:32-36).

Jesus saw it differently and tried to restore the notion of the Sabbath as a gift. Here is a story from Mark:

> One Sabbath Jesus was going through the grain fields; and as they made their way his disciples began to pluck heads of grain. The Pharisees said to him, "Look, why are they doing what is not lawful on the Sabbath?"
>
> And Jesus said to them, "Have you never read what David did when he and his companions were hungry and in need of food? He entered the house of God when Abiathar was high priest and ate the bread of the Presence, which is not lawful for any but the priests to eat, and David gave some to his companions."
>
> Then Jesus said to them, "The Sabbath was made for humankind, not humankind for the Sabbath, so the Son of Man is lord even of the Sabbath."
>
> *Mark 2:23-28*

This is the crucial point: the Sabbath was made for humans, humans were not made for the Sabbath. We should receive the Sabbath as a gift, not as a set of obligatory rules and requirements. It is given to us for rest and refreshment and to make our lives better. It is a day when we do not have to accomplish anything—we can just be. And this can help us become more aware of God and reality and who we really are.

The Sabbath should be a day of leisure. To truly engage in and enjoy leisure, we need to let go of our work and responsibilities and maybe even have some fun; we need to relax and allow our emotional state to rebalance itself. As we let go of the stress, there seems to be a process of replenishment or recharging that takes place below the surface.

But some things can keep us from enjoying these benefits even if we are willing and able to take the day off. Despite our best intentions, we can still be preoccupied with work; we might be worried about a problem, or anticipating the work we need to do or the painful issues we need to face when we return to work. We can find ourselves continually ruminating about our work, and this can make it very difficult to break free of it. And this is especially true if we endure a high level of stress or time pressure such that we cannot finish the work that needs to be done before resting.

It is difficult for some of us to just do nothing. If we are not engaged in something of interest, then our minds turn back to our work. In this case, it can help to find a leisure activity that interests us, one that draws us in. Some psychologists who work in this field talk about fascination. A leisure activity that fascinates us is one that captures our interest and does so naturally and without any effort on our part to direct our attention toward it willfully.

There are other things that can help. Enjoying friendly relationships can help us relax and become more engaged with nonwork activities. So can the freedom to act on our own volition, spontaneously and without seeking the approval or cooperation of others.

It is also a good idea to avoid tightly scheduling our leisure time, if possible. Researchers Gabriela Tonietto and Selin Malkoc provide evidence that if leisure activities are too tightly scheduled, they can feel too much like work and, therefore, might not give us the full benefit of leisure. They advocate what they call rough scheduling. With rough scheduling, we know that we are going to engage in a particular leisure activity and might even look forward to it. But the start and end times are flexible, maybe even a bit spontaneous. That way we are not restricted by a schedule and leisure feels less like work.[59]

I realize that tight scheduling might be necessary for busy people with family or social obligations, and especially for working parents. Sometimes we have to schedule leisure time tightly to meet nonwork commitments.

Maybe we need a Sabbath not just from our work but also from other obligations, if that is possible (it might not be in many cases).

If through the Sabbath our resources are indeed replenished, then when we return to work, we are likely to be stronger, more energetic, and more engaged. And this helps us be more productive and resilient. Our attitude toward our work is more positive.

The Sabbath is an issue not just for us as individuals but also for our organizations. If you are responsible for or have influence over an organization or perhaps a work group, I would encourage you to promote the idea of a Sabbath for your employees and coworkers. Not only is it the right thing to do, but if the members of an organization can return to work refreshed and ready to engage, then the entire organization benefits, including the individuals.

In addition to making Sabbath time available, I would also suggest that you look at what keeps your coworkers and employees from thoroughly enjoying their time off. Is it the always-on email? The enormous time pressures or the stress caused by uncertainty? Whatever it is, if you can start to reduce these factors, you might find that productivity goes up rather than down. And people will be happier.

In any case, I believe that if we take some time off each week and really do let go of our work and our obligations, we will find that the Sabbath is a great gift to us and that it can help us move toward a richer, fuller, less stressful life—the life of shalom. And to this end, I recommend that you think about the next Sunday or whatever day is your next day off and about what you can do to make it a day of rest and refreshment. What would it take for you to actually have a Sabbath that you can enjoy?

The Sabbath can make a big difference if we can find a way to observe it on a regular basis.

Concluding Thoughts About Spiritual Practices

We have discussed a wide variety of spiritual practices with the goal of finding ones that can be integrated into your workday in ways that add meaning and a sense of spiritual connection. Most of the practices in this chapter, with a few exceptions, can be done in just a few minutes during a busy workday; this is important if we are to actually integrate our work and our faith or spirituality during the day. Shorter but nevertheless intense practices can also be done more frequently.

You might experiment with different practices in order to find the ones that seem most appropriate for you. And keep in mind that the ones that are most helpful might change over time and perhaps vary by situation; there is an advantage to becoming familiar with and adopting several different practices.

Becoming more productive in our work is undoubtedly of value and is an objective that is well worth pursuing. But let's also remember that the primary purpose of the spiritual practices is to help us turn our attention toward God, with all this means for our spiritual journey.

Chapter Seven

Can Your Work Be Your Calling?

A calling is a potentially powerful force in our lives. Many of us believe if our work were our calling, we would do it with a greater sense of purpose, passion, and fulfillment. We would find it easier to ride through the challenges and disappointments of our work life and the economic ups and downs that come our way, and we would deal more purposefully with the inevitable stresses and anxieties. We might even enjoy life more.

———————

Most of us would say that a calling feels like something we are meant to do. It will be useful, however, to go further and look at different perspectives, both secular and religious. The concept is richer and more multifaceted than is commonly understood.

I will suggest that calling is a multidimensional concept that reflects our human desire for meaning and purpose. It is grounded in our desire to help other people and contribute to the greater good and—for most of us—to connect with something deeper or larger than ourselves, with God, and to reflect this in our lives. It helps us answer the great existential question "why am I here?"

During times of uncertainty, there may be less talk of finding a calling and more interest in employment security and having a job that pays an acceptable salary. This is certainly understandable. But even in troubled times, having a sense of calling can help us face our challenges and pursue new opportunities with a greater sense of purpose.

———————

Before proceeding, I would like to make several clarifying comments in the hope of avoiding misunderstandings:

1) There have been several articles written by commentators over the last few years concerning the downsides of calling and "following your passion." These have made important points and have provided worthwhile correctives to unrealistic expectations. But in some cases, they have overextended the arguments, even to the point of suggesting that we give up on developing a sense of calling altogether. Despite the pitfalls, developing and acting on a calling can be a very positive experience, bringing with it a more profound sense of purpose.

2) We have to be realistic and acknowledge that finding or developing a sense of calling is not necessarily easy and usually takes time and patience. The journey does not have to be painful or frustrating, however, especially if we have a healthy perspective. I believe the very process of seeking a calling, even when the way forward is clouded in mystery, can be a profound adventure and, in itself, a source of deep meaning and continuing growth. Perhaps in some cases, seeking or developing a calling is meant to be a lifelong journey, accompanied by a growing sense of fulfillment as our understanding evolves and we act accordingly. And sometimes the progress we make on the journey is only apparent when we look back on it.

3) Some of us will find our calling outside of our work, in which case our work will play more of a supporting role—perhaps providing the funds, life support, or skills for a calling that stands apart from our paid work. Maybe we should think in terms of a life calling that incorporates but is not synonymous with our work.

4) At some points in our lives, we might feel called in multiple directions, perhaps in multiple aspects of our lives. Part of developing a calling might involve integrating these into an overarching framework, perhaps involving our faith or spirituality and our deeper identity. Or we might find one particular interest wins out over time. In any case, having a calling does not mean we no longer care about or attend to multiple aspects of our lives.

5) For some people, excessive talk of "following your passion" or seeing your work as your calling can be quite annoying. Some of us work at jobs we do not like in order to serve a purpose apart from the work itself—such as supporting a family, trying to develop a little financial security, or perhaps trying to keep food on the table and a roof over our head. We want to show up, do a good job, get paid, and go home, and understandably do not want to hear lectures about our work having a higher meaning.

A friend refers to "everyday heroes" who go to work at a job that holds no intrinsic meaning for them in order to support a family or meet some other obligation, and I agree with his designation. It can take a great deal of character and perhaps courage to work diligently at something we do not like in order to meet our obligations to a larger purpose. And I can understand why someone would be put off by talk of finding meaning and purpose in their work in this situation.

Even in situations where our job cannot be our calling, we can still hope to draw some satisfaction from understanding how our work contributes to the greater good and the well-being of others. We can also recognize how our work provides the resources that allow us to pursue goals and perhaps a calling outside of our paid work.

We will develop a view of calling using insights from secular, biblical, and historical perspectives, along with contemporary religious commentators. Special attention will be paid to the framework developed by psychologists Bryan Dik and Ryan Duffy, as well as to the importance of expressing our true self in our calling.

We will then take a realistic look at both the benefits and the possible downsides as well as situations where our work cannot and will not be our calling. Finally we will look at ways of developing or perhaps finding a calling for ourselves.

What Do We Mean by Calling?

The concept of calling cuts across multiple disciplines. Some people view it as a purely secular concept and base their understanding in the social sciences. Others view it entirely from a theological perspective and ignore the secular aspects. I believe we need to include both perspectives.

It is true that the language and idea of calling grew out of early Christianity and Judaism. It is also true that most people think of calling (as distinguished from the terms *career* or *occupation*) as having a religious aspect—perhaps its most important aspect. But when we see the concept in purely religious terms and neglect the vital role played by human psychology, we end up with an unnecessarily limited understanding and are therefore unable to access insights and research beyond that provided by religious traditions. The idea becomes disconnected from the broad human quest for meaning and purpose and ceases to apply to people who do not share our religious views.

History

The definition of calling has changed over the years. A thousand years ago, it usually meant being called to an explicitly religious occupation, such as becoming a monk, nun, or priest.

Martin Luther and the reformers in the sixteenth century expanded the concept. Their notion of a Christian calling was no longer confined to the priesthood and religious orders but was now seen as encompassing so-called ordinary work and occupations. The idea was that Christians are called to follow Jesus, obey God's will, and serve others in whatever station they find themselves. These stations could include work and family status. Luther and the others made an exception for inherently sinful occupations, such as pimping, gambling, and thievery, but otherwise saw everyday work as a venue for responding to God's call. Opening the possibility that lay people could experience a divine calling that incorporated their so-called secular work was a big step.

For Luther and, for the most part, sixteenth-century theologian John Calvin, the issue was not a matter of choosing between occupations or stations, but serving God in whatever station one found oneself. Calvin did acknowledge that one could change jobs under certain circumstances, but this was very much a secondary issue. Occupations were semipermanent, reflecting the fact that there was much less opportunity to change jobs in the sixteenth century than there is today, at least for most people. This meant that your current job was your calling. There was an expectation that people would stay in the position that they were born into.

Luther also had an appreciation for the goods and services of various occupations. For example, he spoke of the cobbler knowing that his fellow town folk would be comfortable in the good shoes he had provided. He considered this to be a valid way to serve one's fellow humans and he thereby expanded the common understanding of the Christian call to service. This recognition of the value and contribution of ostensibly nonreligious goods speaks to the importance of our secular work and its contribution to shalom.

The Puritans thought that people have a general calling and a particular calling. The general calling referred to the call of all Christians to follow Jesus and serve others. The particular call had to do with being called to a specific role or task. To a large extent, this thinking was carried forward and continued through much of the Protestant tradition.

Contemporary Views

In 1985, Robert Bellah and a team of sociologists wrote a well-known book based on a series of qualitative interviews called *Habits of The Heart: Individualism and Commitment in American Life*. Bellah proposed that people generally view work in one of three ways:

1. As a job, meaning they primarily exchange time and energy for money, perhaps finding their deeper purpose outside of their work.

2. A career, in other words, a vocation to which they are committed and in which they expect to advance. People in this category derive satisfaction from advancing to higher positions and levels of income, competency, and respect.

3. A calling—work that the individual considers intrinsically important and that provides an opportunity to serve the well-being of others.[60]

Psychologists Amy Wrzesniewski, Paul Rozin, and Gwen Bennett conducted quantitative research that confirmed that people do indeed see their work in one of these three categories and can readily identify the category within which their work fits.[61]

Wrzesniewski also reviewed a broad range of definitions of calling, including both secular and religious. While she acknowledges the historical role of religion, she also believes that the idea of calling has become more secular for most people:

> Callings have largely lost this religious connotation and tend to be defined in the secular sense as consisting of enjoyable or pleasurable work that the individual believes is making the world a better place.[62]

Management scholars Douglas Hall and Dawn Chandler define calling "as work that a person perceives as his purpose in life."[63] They make a similar point as Wrzesniewski and others when they agree that:

> (The concept of calling) has moved away from a religious connotation toward a broader secular view characterized by an individual doing work out of a strong sense of inner direction—work that would contribute to a better world.[64]

They and others maintain that a secular calling comes from within the individual, while a religious calling originates in a belief in God or higher being.[65]

From another secular perspective, management scholars Shoshana Dobrow and Jennifer Tosti-Kharas define calling as a "consuming, meaningful passion people experience toward a domain."[66] Note their emphasis on both passion and the idea that a calling pulls people toward a particular domain, such as music, architecture, or business, rather than one specific job. The domain orientation seems to suggest a degree of flexibility that might allow for further growth. If one is called to the domain of music, for example, one can play a particular instrument as part of this call. But one also has the possibility of broadening the calling to composing, arranging, leading a band, or maybe being a critic or commentator. Feeling a sense of calling to a domain, rather than a particular job, seems to open up the possibility of more varied opportunities.

The Dik and Duffy Framework

Psychologists Bryan Dik and Ryan Duffy have conducted significant research on calling and have written a leading book on the subject: *Make Your Job a Calling: How the Psychology of Vocation Can Change Your Life at Work.*[67]

For one of their studies, Dik and Duffy interviewed 435 college students and 370 adults (a diverse selection of university employees). They found that 68 percent of the students and 62 percent of the adult employees believed that a sense of calling was relevant to their career.[68]

The interviewees, on average, associated calling with three characteristics:

- It originates in a guiding force (either internal or external);
- It should fit their "gifts, passions, and sense of purpose"; and
- It should have "a positive impact on others."[69]

As a result of their work, Dik and Duffy define calling as follows:

> Formally, we define "calling" as a *transcendent summons, experienced as originating beyond the self, to approach a particular life role in a manner oriented toward demonstrating or deriving a sense of purpose or meaningfulness and that holds other-oriented values and goals as primary sources of motivation.*[70]

In other words, a calling:

1. Comes from beyond the person as a transcendent summons (most people would say it comes from God).

2. Demonstrates or provides important meaning for the individual involved.

3. Involves serving others.

Using their survey data and a review of the psychological literature on calling, Dik and Duffy identified two categories of calling in general circulation, distinguished by the source of motivation. Neoclassical callings involve an external source (such as a call from God), while modern callings come from within.[71]

Dik and Duffy argue for the neoclassical model and make several points in support of their position. They find that the idea that calling has lost its religious meaning is not supported by evidence. On the contrary, most of their interviewees think the concept has a religious connotation. They also argue that we should honor the traditional and historical meaning, which is clearly anchored in the idea of a call from God.[72]

I would add that the experience of a transcendent summons can have a great deal of power for the individual involved, potentially outweighing all the other factors and providing a profound sense of purpose. Without this transcendent summons, the term loses much of its power and becomes little more than a construct of human motivation.

This raises an interesting question. If our definition of calling involves what we believe is a transcendent summons, does this mean that one needs to be religious to have a calling? I think not. The attribution and language a person uses does not change the reality of the source.

Expressing Our True Self

I would also place particular emphasis on the idea that an authentic calling should reflect who we are at a deep level, including our deep intrinsic drives and values. You might say that for a calling to be healthy, valid, and life-giving, it needs to be in accord with our true selves, or at least with the person we are meant to become.

Theologically speaking, we might say that we are called by God not just to do something, but to become something—to become the unique person that God intended. Our personal growth and development are an integral part of the larger story; we need to respect and acknowledge our intrinsic values, drives, and identity.

There might be a connection here with Dik and Duffy's observation that with a calling, the person's "sense of purpose and meaning in work" aligns with that of their life as a whole and brings with it a sense of "stability and coherence in life."[73]

This consideration is, I think, the key to understanding why so many well-intentioned, highly motivated people pursue what they believe is a calling only to find themselves burned out and lost a few years later. If our supposed calling does not reflect our authentic self, it is likely to become a deadening experience rather than a life-giving one. This is entirely in line with our earlier discussion of the difference between harmonious and obsessive passion and the critical difference between being driven by internal versus external motivations and values.

James Hillman, psychologist and longtime director of studies at the Jung Institute in Zürich, spoke of what he called the acorn theory. Using the acorn as a metaphor for something which is intended to grow into a fairly specific thing, in this case, an oak tree, Hillman argued that each person "bears a uniqueness that asks to be lived and that is already present before it can be lived."[74]

There are plenty of biblical passages that refer to God forming us before we were born and that would support Hillman's position; I quoted from Psalm 139 earlier. This does not mean that a particular person is specifically designed to become, for example, the chief financial officer of a technology firm, but rather that each individual is designed to become a unique type of person, with unique talents, interests, and values. These unique qualities will manifest themselves in different jobs and roles in different cultures and different situations, but in each culture, there is likely to be a type of job that calls for the particular qualities inherent in the individual.

We might share the view that a valid calling represents a call from God and that it involves contributing to others' well-being. We might also believe that our social setting and interactions can help us develop and define our calling. Nevertheless, if what we think of as our calling does not also represent our deeper selves, and contribute to our own healthy personal development, then I believe it will not be sustainable and will probably lead to burnout and disillusionment. It is likely to become deadening, rather than life-giving and energizing.

————

Some might say that placing a high value on our inner motivation means we are only interested in the selfish pursuit of "self-actualization." Others would say that this orientation neglects the well-being of others. The underlying logic of this type of criticism seems to conflate a desire to be true to ourselves with sins such as self-aggrandizement and excessive selfishness. On the contrary, I believe proper respect for one's own values and drives is more likely to lead to a concern for others than to selfish behavior.

The argument depends on how we view the human person at the deepest level. Let's suppose, for the sake of argument, that we believe that the individual and human nature are corrupt to the point where, without social pressure and controls, people cannot help but proceed based on sinful motives. In that case, we are likely to think that we need to keep ourselves in check, usually through social controls, and be highly distrustful of our internal motivations.

But I do not buy it. I have seen too many people who want to do good and are sincerely grieved when they fall short. Sin is almost always present, of course, as is temptation, but it seems more like a tarnish that hides our true selves than a fundamental aspect of our deepest nature. And we have strong, personal evidence of this; most of us feel bad, or at least uncomfortable, when we harm others, even if the result is of material benefit to ourselves. And most of us feel good when we have helped others, even if it requires personal sacrifice.

This raises a related issue. What of the artist or musician who is passionately dedicated to expressing something within them, or the scientist dedicated to new discovery, or scholars dedicated to exploring an arcane subject of no apparent significance? In some cases, there can be an altruistic motive, such as the artist hoping people will enjoy his or her work. But not always. In some cases, there is no such motive—the sole motive seems to be the joy of creating, of self-expression, or of discovery.

Are these people not following a calling because they are not consciously trying to contribute to the well-being of others?

In some cases, people in these situations do make important contributions. They wind up creating art or music that thousands or millions enjoy, or they make a discovery that eventually leads to unexpected applications of great benefit. Perhaps there is an unconscious desire for the greater good, despite appearances to the contrary.

Or perhaps individuals have been given something deep within that wants to be expressed. Perhaps as we express something of our true selves, we are contributing to the blossoming of human culture, making the world a richer place, and maybe even expressing something of God. We might be designed to contribute to the common good without realizing it.

It is possible, of course, that what we think of as self-expression or the search for knowledge is really nothing more than a reflection of more base motives. But I remain confident that most of us can tell the difference most of the time, if we pay attention.

Benefits of a Calling

Working with a sense of calling can have substantial benefits. Most of us would expect to work with a greater degree of purpose, fulfillment, and satisfaction. I would expect that we would also be more productive, energized, and resilient.

There have been quite a few research studies that seem to confirm this. From the research, it appears that following a calling is associated with work that is more meaningful and satisfying. People who work with a sense of calling tend to be more committed to their work and their organization, have greater clarity of purpose, and are more likely to experience greater meaning and satisfaction in their life overall.[75]

We need to draw a critical distinction, however. There is evidence that it is not perceiving the calling that provides these benefits, but acting on it. People who do not act on their perceived calling are not likely to experience more meaning and satisfaction in their work than those who do not perceive a calling. Moreover, the sense of calling increases and deepens as we live into it.[76]

Implications for the Organization

Calling is not only an individual issue; there are very real benefits for an organization if a larger proportion of its members see their involvement in this way. This applies to both paid and unpaid work.

But leaders should recognize that it is the individual who decides if their work is indeed a calling, not the leader. It is not a matter of pep talks or exhortation—only the individual can determine if and how their work fits their values and motivation.

There can be a contagion factor, however. If more employees see their work as a calling, their positive attitude and performance are likely to have a positive effect on others. This can apply to teams; if a majority of the team members see their involvement as a calling, then the team is likely to be more productive, have greater collaboration and less conflict, and generate fewer complaints of missed deadlines or unsatisfactory performance by members of the team. Unfortunately, the reverse can also be true; if the members do not have a sense of calling or at least some sense of purpose, then team performance is likely to suffer.

The organization needs to approach this issue with integrity. It is too easy for employees to develop the sense that talk of having a calling is just another tool to motivate them to do more for the company. This is likely to lead to resistance rather than engagement. Leaders can talk of the organization's mission and contribution to the greater good, the importance of individual tasks, and their appreciation for coworkers. They can also try to improve the fit between workers and the work. But they should leave the question of calling to the individuals.

What If My Work Cannot Be My Calling?

We have to acknowledge that no matter how hard they try, some people will not perceive a calling in their work. So what can they do in this case? If they cannot change jobs, then I would suggest that there are several types of responses.

Management professors Justin Berg, Amy Wrzesniewski and Jane Dutton observed that individuals sometimes have flexibility in how they do their jobs and that, in some cases, they might be able to bring their jobs into closer alignment with their values and thereby find more meaning in them. They called this job crafting and suggested that this can involve task crafting (modifying the work itself), relationship crafting, or cognitive crafting (reframing or redefining how we think of the task). Each of these has the potential to bring our work more in line with our values and drives.[77] While this is not the perfect solution and might not always be possible, it can help in some cases.

In addition to job crafting, professors Adam Grant, Justin Berg, and Victoria Johnson introduced the idea of leisure crafting—developing or reorienting leisure activities that fulfill a sense of calling the individuals cannot satisfy in their paid work.[78] People can apply leisure crafting, for instance, to charity work and hobbies. In these cases, our paid work can still play an essential role by letting us develop the resources needed to support the unpaid calling.

If our work is seen by us as a job or career, to use Bellah's terms, but not a calling, we can still develop a sense of meaning. Even if we are only working because we need (or want) the money, we can still think about why the money is important to us; this can be an important source of meaning.

And in any case, perhaps we should think of a life calling. Our work can either be a central part of this or it can play an essential supporting role.

Downsides

Are there downsides to seeing our work as a calling? Perhaps. There are plenty of stories of people who begin a career enthusiastically in the belief they have been called but then, a few years later, find themselves burned out. We can also be in situations where we have become obsessed with our work to the point that we have trouble leaving it behind, enjoying leisure, or maintaining healthy relationships.

I would argue that a true calling should be life-giving and energizing, by definition, and should not lead to burnout. But there are issues of which we should be aware.

In a study by organizational behavior scholars Teresa Cardador and Brianna Caza, the authors compared what they thought of as healthy and unhealthy callings (generally defined by the work's effect on personal relationships). They made a strong case that a critical issue is what they called work-identity flexibility. As they put it:

> Without work-identity flexibility, individuals with callings have more difficulty adapting to the natural changes and stressors in their profession, lives, and work environment.[79]

I interpret their conclusions to mean that while there are significant benefits to experiencing a sense of calling in our work, we need to be careful not to identify too closely with a particular job, position, or accomplishment. Letting our self-identity be too dependent on these things can lead to brittleness and negatively affect our relationships. We must be able to lose any of these and still have the flexibility to move forward without losing our identity or sense of calling.

Earlier we discussed Vallerand's dual passion model. I would argue that harmonious passion is consistent with a true calling, while obsessive passion is not and that brittleness is more likely to be associated with obsessive passion.

It is not so easy to distinguish where harmonious passion ends and obsessive passion begins. We should be mindful of the risk that our passion can become obsessive, almost without us realizing it. A true calling should reflect harmonious passion; it should be life-giving and energizing, allow us to experience healthy relationships, and, in general, to feel as though we are becoming our true selves as we contribute to the well-being of society.

Dobrow has raised the possibility that a strong sense of calling could, in some circumstances, lead to tunnel vision.[80] We might become so focused on our own calling that we lose sight of other important priorities and values, such as personal relationships and the work of others. It might also lead us to ignore or devalue work that does not directly relate to our calling.

There is also the possibility that following a calling, and being too committed to it, can lead us to make unwise decisions—for example, ones with seriously negative financial consequences. The impracticality can be in the eyes of the beholder, however. Taking a financial loss, or a pay cut, to pursue a calling involves a trade-off that should be made by the individuals and families involved. But we need to be clear-eyed about it. We can imagine situations where someone has put their family in grave financial risk to pursue what they believe is a calling without thinking through the consequences.

None of this is to deny that a calling can be a beautiful thing, for the reasons discussed. But there is a role for discernment. Spiritual practices, such as prayer, can help us here. So can considering the teachings of Jesus and how they apply to what we are doing—not in a demanding, heavy-handed way, but in a way that leads to a fuller life.

How Do We Develop a Calling?

We often speak of "finding" our calling as though it is a matter of looking for the right job or role. Some scholars, such as Tod Bolsinger of Fuller Theological Seminary, have argued that a calling is not found but formed or developed.[81]

The process is most likely a combination of both seeking and developing. We search by exploring different options, looking for a good fit between ourselves, the work, and the social environment. But the sense of calling also develops as we engage and experience different activities, develop our talents, and learn more about our interests.

For our purposes here, and to simplify the demands on the language, I will refer to *developing* a calling, while recognizing that there are also elements of search involved.

Developing a calling will almost always take a lot of time, patience, trial and error, and reflection. Maybe some people experience a sudden revelation, a bolt out of the blue, so to speak, that sets them on their course, but this is unusual. Experiencing a sense of divine summons can dominate our thinking about our calling, but it almost always takes time for this experience to develop. There seems to be a need for a prolonged negotiation between our authentic selves and the environment.

Active Discernment

Dik, Duffy, and Brandy Eldridge distinguish between active and passive discernment.[82] Passive discernment might involve waiting for a sense of inspiration before acting, and is less likely to provide insight.

With active discernment, as we engage in different activities, and reflect on and explore our interests, we begin to understand which ones seem to have deeper meaning for us. We also start noticing those aspects of our work that we especially enjoy and to which we are drawn; this can also apply to leisure activities.

We might find ourselves drawn to an activity that seems to have no possible connection with a calling but still seems to be a source of joy and satisfaction. Later on, with the benefit of hindsight, we might be able to see how developing the talent involved in the supposedly inconsequential activity eventually proved essential to a calling that emerged later. It can be important to notice and let these talents develop and grow.

The development process is complicated by the fact that it involves multiple levels. Are we called to a particular job? Or in a general direction? And does the sense of calling change over time? We want the call to be specific and concrete, to be to a particular job in a particular place and time, but this is not necessarily how it works. While the general direction might be clear and compelling, the specific job might be less so and might change over time in response to varied and changing circumstances.

Our life stage has a lot to do with this. Even if I had the same sense of calling when I was in my twenties as I do now, the opportunities then were quite different.

Serving Others

Most definitions of calling recognize the importance of contributing to others' well-being and perhaps to society as a whole. This seems to be a necessary condition for most of us if our work is to have a significant sense of purpose.

We should pay attention to those things that we have a strong desire to change. This does not mean we should move straight from feelings to action; situations can be complicated and solutions hard to find. We have all seen situations where action based on feelings, and not reason, has made situations worse rather than better. If we are truly called to solve a complicated problem, we need to be willing to spend the time and energy to study the situation before acting impulsively.

Gifts

As is widely understood, our particular gifts play an important role. Guidance counselors, human resource professionals, managers, and churches have spent considerable time trying to help people discern their gifts so they can be matched with the right job or set of tasks, including volunteer tasks. People will be more effective, happier, and motivated when they are using their gifts in productive ways.

Gifts do not stand alone, however. We are better at some types of activities than at others, but we also develop abilities and talents as we move and work in particular directions, especially if these directions involve our passion. If we act on them, our deep desires play a formative role in the development of new gifts.

Experience in a variety of situations, with much trial and error, can help us develop an understanding of our current and potential gifts. Sometimes it can also help if we obtain the opinions of others after they have had an opportunity to work with us. In any case, having a better understanding of these gifts is not the whole story, but it can certainly help us discern our most appropriate direction.

Personal Reflection and Spiritual Practices

The experience we gain as we take action should be combined with reflection. Ideally, after engaging in work, we reflect on our experience and what this might tell us about the direction we should be moving. This reflection can occur in a community (such as in a small group) or solitude; there are advantages to each.

The spiritual practice of Examen described in Chapter Six can be a big help. As you reflect on your activities, when did you feel like you were moving in the right direction? Were there times when you might even have felt like you were moving with God or were spiritually inspired? These experiences can provide critical clues.

As we reflect on our current and past engagement with work, there are questions we can use to prompt reflection. For example, we can consider what seems to give meaning to our lives and how our work might connect with this. Dik and Duffy propose asking questions like the following:

1. "When it comes down to it, what ultimately is most important in life?"

2. "How would you describe your overall purpose in life?"

3. "Where do you try to find answers to questions of purpose and meaningfulness?"[83]

These questions could lead to other big questions: What gives your life and your work meaning? How does your work connect to or support the meaning you find in life? In addition to reflecting on these questions and your answers to them, you could also combine them with prayer, asking for guidance, and listening to the spirit moving within you.

These are not easy questions to answer. But they do not need to be answered definitively. Just spending serious time reflecting on them can move us in the right direction.

Joy as a Signpost

I would add at least one more question: What gives you a sense of deep joy?

Joy might be the most important signpost on the way to developing a healthy sense of call. By joy, I do not mean happiness, or even delirious happiness. Joy is characterized by a deep sense that we are inspired and moving in the right direction. I believe it is also an essential spiritual signpost.

What brings you joy?

Chapter Eight

Spiritual Dimensions of Leadership

Leaders face unique challenges and carry heavy burdens; being in a leadership position can feel like being in a pressure cooker. But while the burdens are great, there can also be an exhilarating sense of contributing to the greater good, achieving a new level of personal growth, and helping others to thrive.

While much of the material developed in the preceding chapters applies to leaders as well as to others, the issues can become more intense for the leader, whether we are speaking of the pain of stress, the role of spiritual practices, the need for character strengths, the temptations of sin, or the challenge of staying connected to our deeper purpose.

The need for competent, virtuous leadership is especially critical during times of crisis. During these times, there can be a particularly stark contrast between honest, effective leadership, and weak, dishonest, or foolish leadership.

This chapter will explore the spiritual aspects of leadership and look for ways that leaders can tap into the deep resources of their own faith or spirituality to find support and guidance. I begin by looking at the inner world of the leader, and especially what distinguishes leaders from others.

Abraham Zaleznik and the Inner Life of Leaders

The late Abraham Zaleznik heavily influenced my thinking. In his classic *Harvard Business Review* article "Managers and Leaders: Are They Different?"[84] Zaleznik argued that leaders, as compared to managers, are deeply dissatisfied with reality as it is and are committed to changing

153

it. Managers, on the other hand, are generally satisfied with reality and prioritize conserving structures, preventing problems, and balancing conflicting forces.

According to Zaleznik:

> (Leaders are) active instead of reactive, shaping
> ideas instead of responding to them. Leaders adopt a
> personal and active attitude toward goals.[85]

Leaders use the tools at their disposal to shape people's thinking, orientation, and expectations in order to establish the vision of the organization and set its direction.

On the other hand, managers have a less personal attitude toward goals, and:

> ... tend to view work as an enabling process involving
> some combination of people and ideas interacting to
> establish strategies and make decisions. They help the
> process along by calculating the interests in opposition,
> planning when controversial issues should surface, and
> reducing tensions.[86]

I interpret this to mean that managers are more focused on keeping the organization and its processes operating smoothly while minimizing surprises and disruptions. Leaders and managers might use the same or similar tools in some cases, and successful leaders might need strong management skills, but the underlying motivation is quite different.

Zaleznik borrowed early twentieth-century philosopher and psychologist William James's terminology of once-born and twice-born personalities, though he used it for different purposes. For Zaleznik, once-born people have become generally reconciled to their environment and social relationships and tend to prioritize maintaining order and moving forward in a controlled, predictable manner. The twice-born are much less reconciled and focus on changing the status quo and are often bored with the mundane tasks of management. Managers are much more likely to be once-born; leaders are likely to be twice-born.[87]

The intense personal commitment to an outcome chosen and internalized by the leader is the key to defining what it means to be a leader. This commitment can reflect a profound dissatisfaction with things as they are, but perhaps we should broaden this a bit to include personal commitments to defend the status quo in the face of an undesirable change that would otherwise occur. And perhaps this commitment is not limited to goals that the leader brings with them to their position of leadership but can also include ones that develop as they appraise and interact with their new environment.

There are other definitions of "leader" from which we could choose. One popular definition is that leaders are people who have followers; this is implicit in much of the literature about leaders. A related idea is that leaders are people who influence others. While these ideas contain some truth, I resist them because they ignore the leader's inner motivation and commitment. A person might have a great many loyal employees, high status, popularity, and fame, but that does not mean that they are a leader.

An advantage of Zaleznik's approach is that it distinguishes leaders from highly successful managers. By focusing on the leader's motivation, it separates leaders from people who find themselves in positions of authority over large numbers of people, and who are very competent and valuable managers, but who nevertheless do not have a passionate personal commitment to a chosen outcome.

Zaleznik believed that managers are more likely than leaders to be promoted by large organizations. This certainly seemed to be true of the large corporations for which I worked back when Zaleznik was doing his research. The situation might be changing, however, due to the changing business environment and the instability of markets. I have not been employed by a large corporation for more than thirty years, but I have worked closely with ones that have been my customers and suppliers. My impression is that there are now more people who qualify as leaders under Zaleznik's definition than there were before.

An inference we might draw from Zaleznik's approach is that despite the cultural image of the successful leader, leaders on average might have lower prospects of success than managers. Given the leader's personal commitment to change reality, he or she might be more likely to forgo conventional success and more willing to take risks than are managers. Leaders are consequently more likely to flame out.

Good leaders are important, but so are good managers. We saw this in the early days of the COVID-19 crisis. There was certainly an obvious need for effective leadership at all levels. But behind the scenes, there was also a heightened need for effective management as many businesses and medical organizations faced critical supply-chain challenges. I saw this first hand on a video meeting a few weeks into the pandemic as representatives of several large corporations described the complexities of their supply chains and the steps they were taking to ensure timely delivery from hundreds of direct suppliers, many with multiple layers of subcontractors. While I think it is essential to differentiate the roles of managers and leaders, we need both.

––––––––

Both leaders and managers need to know themselves and have a firm understanding of their goals, both personal and organizational. For leaders, identifying their mission can be very personal, flowing as it does from their personal commitment. He or she must have a good understanding of themselves and the outcome they seek. Clarity is essential; there must be more than just general dissatisfaction and desire for change. Acting on a vague desire for change is not likely to lead to success.

Time spent in prayer and reflection can help us move in the direction of clarity. Taking a step back and letting go of our immediate concerns, and then thinking about our values, our connection to a greater reality, and our deeper purpose can help us seek clarity as to our primary goals. And this can help us act in the face of the risks inherent in leadership.

Toxic Leadership

When we consider the change a leader is trying to bring about, we hope that their intention is to contribute to the greater good. This is often the case; most people, including leaders, find considerable meaning and satisfaction in contributing to the greater good.

Alas, though, this is not always the case. Sin, and sinful motivations, can enter into the process and corrupt the leader.

Of particular importance for leaders is the issue of narcissism. Here I turn to the work of psychoanalyst and leadership scholar Manfred Kets de Vries.

Most people (including me) think of narcissism as "excessive self-love or egocentrism,"[88] to use the definition provided by the American Psychological Association.

Kets de Vries and co-author Elisabet Engellau distinguish between constructive and reactive narcissism. With constructive narcissism, leaders might be ambitious and want to change reality, but they can still be well-balanced, work well with other people, be introspective, have empathy, and take advice and collaborate.[89]

Kets de Vries and Engellau suggest that a small dose of narcissism can be healthy in that it can provide the leader with "a foundation for conviction about the righteousness of their cause" and a belief in the special mission of their organization.[90] This can be energizing for the organization.

There are risks, however. They also point out that "narcissism is a toxic drug." If we are not careful, it can be disastrous to combine the power and pressures of leadership with a "narcissistic disposition."[91]

Here and in much of his other work, Kets de Vries writes as a psycho-analyst and is able to discuss toxic narcissism as originating in human relationships, especially negative ones, formed during childhood.[92] While his psychoanalytic approach is more than we can cover here, we can nevertheless be alert to the fact that our subconscious drives can affect how we act as leaders.

The problem is not self-confidence, strength of will, or so-called charisma. The problem with reactive narcissism is that it diverts one's power, attention, and energy away from worthwhile goals and toward one's ego needs. Reactive narcissism can result in leaders who, in the words of Kets de Vries and Engellau:

> ... become fixated on issues of power, status, prestige, and superiority. To them, life turns into a zero-sum game: there are winners and losers. They are preoccupied with looking out for number one.[93]

As a result, the leader's work, mission, and leadership practices become focused on meeting their own needs, not on bringing about constructive change. This makes them much less effective and might even cause great harm. It is hard to imagine their work being life-giving for themselves or inspiring to others.

The problem goes beyond that of leaders with a particular tendency toward narcissism. With power frequently comes the temptation to look after one's selfish desires to an unacceptable level. As we frequently see in politics, institutional guardrails are often necessary to protect us from leaders who might otherwise misuse their power.

Other Problems

Narcissism is not the only potential spiritual or moral problem for leaders.

Some leaders have engaged in behavior that involves bullying, over-the-top rudeness, the deliberate creation of strife, and sexual harassment. These are so obviously wrong that I do not have anything to add about them.

There are other behaviors that are not so obviously evil but nevertheless work against the needs of the people and the goals of the organization. These can involve:

- Poor communication and a lack of transparency
- A lack of support in the form of tools and training
- Unintentional favoritism
- Relative disinterest in less important members
- Overmanagement that stifles initiative
- Autocratic or top-down decision-making

Some of these can be in the eye of the beholder, at least some of the time, but they often also reflect poor management.

But there is another issue that might come into play. I suggested earlier that it is the intense personal commitment to a goal that distinguishes the leader. Within the context of an organization, this commitment is healthy when it involves inspiring and involving other members of the organization in the willing pursuit of a common goal. It is possible, however, for the intensity of the commitment to result in the leader seeing people in exclusively instrumental terms—in other words, seeing them solely in terms of what they can do for the achievement of the leader's goals. The relationship between leader and follower ceases to be one of authenticity, mutual respect, and dignity, and becomes unhealthy. Paradoxically, the leader's intense commitment becomes counterproductive for his or her goal.

This possible problem is not necessarily inherent in the leader's level of commitment; it is more a corruption of their commitment. For leadership to be healthy over the long-term, the leader needs to remain appreciative of the worth and dignity of individuals, whether they have significant practical value to the leader or not.

Moral Development

Moral development can hold the key. Building on the work of Robert Kegan and others, leadership scholar Bruce Avolio came to the conclusion that "the Holy Grail of leadership was establishing and developing the moral center in leaders, and of course in those they led." This moral center leads to a higher perspective and the ability to get past the question of "what's in it for me."[94] It seems to me that such leaders are more likely to find the deeper meaning of their work. They are also likely to be more effective.

I would say that Avolio's idea of moral development might have a spiritual or religious connection. At its best, Christianity, for example, encourages the character strengths that represent this moral development, especially integrity, compassion, humility, and prudence, as previously noted. It offers examples and practices that help in the development process. And it promotes a sense of transcendent purpose. Inherent in this is the second commandment—to love our neighbors as ourselves.

The earlier discussion of the difference between harmonious and obsessive passion is worth remembering here, too. We would expect a leader's harmonious passion to be life-giving and positive and lead to more effective leadership. On the other hand, as leadership scholars Melissa Trivisonno and Julian Barling point out, obsessive passion in a leader leads in a very different direction: "motivated by the need to feel socially accepted and to protect one's self-worth," obsessive passion can lead to "a relentless pursuit of and unhealthy involvement in the goal at hand, with leaders failing to establish reasonable expectations."[95] This implies that obsessive leadership is more likely to lead to tyrannical behavior, over-control of subordinates, weak relationships, and, once again, burnout. The probable connection of narcissism to obsession is obvious.

A leader's inner life and spiritual formation are important factors in the health of their psyche, their effectiveness as leaders, the well-being and engagement of their followers, and the prospects of fulfilling their mission. Developing an increasingly deep faith or spirituality can be important for the leader.

Building the Shalomic Organization

While the leader can set the organization's goals, the likelihood of meeting these goals is dependent on other people, most notably the leader's followers.[96] You might say that the leader has to be concerned with both the mission and the people who are to carry out the mission.

There are plenty of books on leadership techniques and, in fact, most material written about leadership focuses on how to be effective as a leader (and as a manager). I do not intend to cover the same ground, and in any case, readers will probably be familiar with some of these books and will have their own ideas.

More important to our discussion, at this point, is the idea of what I call the shalomic organization. We discussed the biblical concept of shalom as a sort of holistic flourishing involving multiple dimensions, among them the spiritual, interpersonal, economic, relational, societal, psychological, and work-related aspects of our lives. This raises a question: what would shalom look like in a large, modern organization like a corporation? And what would leadership look like in a shalomic organization?

I would define the shalomic organization as one that embodies and promotes multidimensional human flourishing within the organization itself and among its members, *and* contributes to flourishing in the broader society through the products or services it provides. Shalomic leadership involves moving the organization in this direction.

There can be a tendency to see shalom primarily in terms of interpersonal relations and maybe in terms of spiritual and emotional well-being. These qualities are very good, and are indeed part of shalom, but we also need to include the concept of material well-being. Business organizations exist to provide goods and services for the welfare of society (and for which people are willing to pay) and to generate the revenue necessary for the well-being of the members and investors in the business organization. Businesses need to produce goods that are valued by the market and do so in a way that creates value in the form of profits; this is the foundation of the business's ability to provide for its participants' material well-being.

I suggested earlier that material well-being and prosperity are valued elements of the biblical concept of shalom but are often overlooked in discussions of the Bible. We should be careful that our understanding of the shalomic organization does not make the same mistake.

When we speak of productivity, a key goal of shalomic leadership is to establish an environment where people can thrive as they contribute as active participants to the organization's goals. Most people are happier in their work lives when they are more purposeful, engaged, and creative; they are also likely to be more productive. Leaders can either encourage these characteristics or suppress them; their choice can have a great effect on the organization's success.

Paradoxically, in some ways, the shalomic organization requires more, not less, of the leader. Even though authority and initiative tend to be forced downward in the shalomic organization, providing opportunity for more agency and initiative throughout it, the leader still has the primary responsibility to establish the mission of the organization and inspire and motivate others to share in this mission. This might seem more difficult as the leader becomes less controlling.

Success in this situation also depends on the leader finding and developing people who can thrive in this environment. The members who respond to this type of leadership can grow and develop their capabilities, sense of efficacy, and confidence. By being respected, they are likely to work with a greater sense of purpose as they develop deeper congruence between their own intrinsic values, motivation, and goals, and those of the organization. They are also likely to build community as they work with others to pursue common goals in an environment that respects their dignity. Such an organization is also likely to be more effective and meet with success in the market.

Human Dignity as a Central Concern

An appreciation for the dignity of all individuals underlies the shalomic organization. Recall the two great creation stories. Humans are made in God's image in the first story and become human when the spirit of God is breathed into them in the second. This suggests that people have a fundamental dignity and therefore deserve our respect, no matter their social or economic status. This respect for human dignity is an essential aspect of the biblical understanding of shalom and has a lot to do with the shalomic organization.

This respect and dignity go beyond kindness and generosity. While the latter virtues are important and necessary, respect for human dignity goes further and includes respecting the agency of people at work. Earlier I talked about different manufacturing plants I had seen and the importance of respecting the dignity of workers and allowing them to bring their talent to the job. It is not always possible, but when we can put people into positions where they can use their initiative and creativity, we are more likely to move toward shalom, for everyone's benefit.

In my experience, not everyone responds well to the opportunity to become more engaged and responsible, but most do. And most will respond to the opportunity to become a more shalomic organization. Not all jobs can be redesigned to accommodate human nature to the extent I would like. But most organizations can move farther in this direction.

Respecting human dignity also has implications for goal congruence within the organization. Having a sense of common purpose does not mean that everyone has to have the same personal goals or even the same philosophy or ideology; these should be left to the individual. But we would like coworkers to find enough congruence with the organization's goals to willingly share in the organization's purpose in a way that is meaningful to them and productive for the organization.

The Value of Faith and Spirituality for Leaders

The rich resources of our faith and our faith traditions can help us develop the depth of perspective, character, and equanimity necessary to carry the burdens of leadership. The resources that I believe are particularly valuable for leaders include the following:

1. ***Spiritual practices*** such as prayer and meditation can help us turn our attention to God and, over time, develop a more profound sense of mission and purpose. These practices can energize us, help us work with a greater sense of purpose and effectiveness, calm our emotions in times of crisis, and help us stay focused on the work in front of us.

2. ***Theology*** can provide a broader, deeper perspective that transcends our current difficulties. By its nature, theology directs our attention toward God and transcendent reality and reminds us of who we really are.

3. Faith can help us develop what we think of as ***character***. Honesty, goodwill, courage, equanimity, and humility are all critical for leaders—especially in times of crisis—and are virtues promoted and encouraged by our faith and faith institutions.

4. Our faith or spirituality can help us find ***meaning and purpose*** in our lives, including our work lives. Religion and theology are largely meaning-making enterprises; discerning the more profound meaning in our organizational mission can help us find the strength to persevere and the wisdom to act with clarity.

Churches, seminaries, and other religious entities can offer opportunities to engage in spiritual practices (especially contemplative practices) as preparation for action. They can help us develop a transcendent perspective that supplies meaning to our ongoing work. And they can help us see the positive, practical value of what we think of as the traditional virtues.

The Bible is full of stories and insights about leadership, many of which were developed during extreme crises. Think of the great Elijah in the wilderness finding strength and courage in the face of exhaustion and fear; the virtuous David becoming a powerful leader, committing a great sin, and finally groping his way forward toward redemption; or Ezra, Nehemiah, and the later Isaiah leading their people through the challenges of rebuilding a ruined civilization. Or think of Jesus facing the ultimate existential crisis and, in the process, launching his previously fickle followers on a radically new course.

Spending time in prayer and other spiritual practices and being open to our intuitions and spiritual promptings can help us move toward clarity, especially when combined with reflection. Spiritual practices can also help us cultivate the humility it takes to listen to others, observe the business and social environment, and challenge our assumptions. These are necessary if we are to develop a sufficiently accurate view of reality.

Leaders must act on their own responsibility, at least part of the time. This requires a clear ethical framework, perhaps driven by their faith or spirituality. Taking the initiative in uncertain circumstances requires some of the character strengths discussed earlier, especially courage, hope, optimism, and resilience.

Character also matters when it comes to enlisting people in the mission. We discussed the role of character and religious virtues in helping to develop the trust and collaborative relationships necessary for success. This is true for everyone in the organization, but especially for leaders; who wants to follow a leader they cannot trust or who lacks character?

And proper respect for the dignity of each individual as an image-bearer of God is essential.

————

Leaders often have to carry heavy burdens; these require a considerable degree of spiritual maturity.

But as painful and burdensome as leadership can be at times, for the true leader the only alternative is to be less faithful to their calling and their true nature; this means hiding from the person they are meant to be and the challenges they are meant to confront.

And accepting these burdens is often what it takes to move society forward toward shalom.

Conclusion

I believe our work could be much better and by this I mean more purposeful, fulfilling, and maybe even more enjoyable, and that tapping into the resources of our faith or spirituality can make an important difference. I hope this book has been helpful and has encouraged you to explore how your own faith or spirituality can inform and support you in your work.

I have attempted to describe an approach to Christian spirituality that can be applied to our contemporary work lives. Underlying this spirituality are two deep intuitive desires: 1) to experience a deeper sense of connection with God and the divine mystery, and 2) to contribute to the greater good and the well-being of other people. Bringing these to the surface helps us see and experience the sacred meaning of our everyday work.

We have covered a great deal of territory, ranging from biblical theology as it pertains to work and flourishing to the practical issues we face. Along the way, we have discussed spiritual practices that can help us turn toward God during the workday, the biblical concept of shalom, obstacles like sin and adversity, the development of character, and special topics such as calling and the spiritual dimension of leadership.

Our work is important and so is our faith or spirituality. If we can integrate these in a way that respects and values both dimensions, then our experience of work and spirituality can be richer and more fulfilling.

I hope you will continue to reflect on the sacred meaning of your own work in light of your own faith or spirituality and your own experiences of work.

Appendices

Appendix A

Work in the Bible

Introduction

The Bible has a great deal to say about work and how it contributes, or should contribute, to human well-being. This section pulls together what I believe are some of the most essential work-related insights the Bible offers. It will review the biblical view of the relationship among God, humans, and work, the goal of shalom and human flourishing, the rules and guidelines for work, the consequences of not following the rules and guidelines, wisdom for the individual worker, and the work-related teachings of Jesus and the New Testament.

Many of these passages can be found in the main chapters of the book; others are additions. I am including both in order to provide a more comprehensive resource.

Foundation: The Relationship of God, Humans, and Work

The two great creation stories at the beginning of the Bible (Genesis 1:1-2:3 and Genesis 2:3–3:24) provide a foundational view of the relationship between God and humans and the role of humans and human work in creation. While the two stories are quite different in some ways, they also make similar points.

In both stories, God is fully sovereign and the creator of all that is. The first story begins "in the beginning when God created the heavens and the earth…" (Genesis 1:1), the second "in the day that the LORD God made the earth and the heavens…" (Genesis 2:4). In both stories, what God creates is good and appears to be an expression of his goodness.

There is a close connection between God and the humans he creates. In the first story, God creates humans in his image (Genesis 1:26–27). People can debate what "the image of God" actually means, but the language certainly implies that God has given an important degree of agency to humans. Moreover they are to have dominion, be fruitful and multiply, and fill the earth. While the Hebrew word for "create" is not used for human work in the Bible, this passage does suggest that humans are to develop and produce value using that which God has provided. And it is fair to say that this applies to both individuals and their communities. God has given humans agency and is working through them.

The imagery in the second story is different, but the message is similar. God shapes the first human out of the dust, but it is not a conscious human being until God breathes his spirit into him:

> … then the LORD God formed man from the dust of
> the ground, and breathed into his nostrils the breath (or
> spirit) of life; and the man became a living being.
> Genesis 2:7

God then places the now living human into the garden "to till it and keep it" (Genesis 2:15) and to give names to all living things (Genesis 2:19–20). Here, too, humans are given agency and the opportunity and responsibility to work and produce.

Here and elsewhere, there is a strong sense that God designed each of us, maybe for a particular purpose, and knows us better than we know ourselves. There are, for example, several allusions to God forming us before we were born; see, for example, Psalm 139:13-16, Jeremiah 1:5, Job 10:8-11, Isaiah 49:1, and Galatians 1:15.

Despite the inherent goodness of creation, humans are nevertheless to participate in completing it through their work. We see this in the above reference to the human role of tilling and keeping the garden (Genesis 2:15).[98] The nature of God's provision is another illustration of this. God provides, but it is up to humans to work to convert this provision into useful products. We can find an example of this in Psalm 104:14–15, where God provides grass, and people are to work to bring forth from this wine, oil, and bread.

The use of metaphors like being made in God's image, filled with God's spirit, and designed and known by God in the womb suggest that humans have a fundamental dignity that does not depend on circumstances of life or social hierarchy. There is something special about each human that should be respected and allowed to grow as God intended, without being unduly suppressed.

Work, Shalom, and Human Flourishing

The Bible speaks positively of human flourishing and often has material well-being and prosperity in sight when it does so. These are included in the biblical concept of shalom, a sort of multidimensional human flourishing that includes our relationship with God, friendly relations with others, contentment, peace of mind, the end of hostilities, prosperity, material well-being, good health, and life itself. These aspects of shalom all work together.

Our relationships with God and with humans are at the center of shalom, but this does not mean that the Bible discounts the importance of prosperity and material well-being; these are an integral part of shalom. This is made clear in several places. God blessed Abraham and his family with flocks, herds, silver, gold, camels, donkeys, and descendants (Genesis 24:35). The Israelites will come out of Egypt with "great possessions" (Genesis 15:14). God will bless those who follow his rules with children, fruit, grape, wine, oil, cattle flocks, land, good health, and security (Deuteronomy 7:12-15). Flowing streams, wheat, barley, fig trees, pomegranates, honey, iron, and copper are included in the list of blessings (Deuteronomy 8:6-10; see also Leviticus 26:3-6, Deuteronomy 11:13-15, Deuteronomy 28:1-6, Joshua 24:13, Proverbs 10:22, and Isaiah 65:21). Prosperity is frequently noted as an essential part of the shalom for which people hope (Psalm 72:3, Isaiah 48:18).

Of course, we must not idolize prosperity; it is not permanent and can disappear quickly:

> *Do not wear yourself out to get rich;*
> *be wise enough to desist.*
> *When your eyes light upon it, it is gone;*
> *for suddenly it takes wings to itself,*
> *flying like an eagle toward heaven.*
>
> Proverbs 23:4–5

See also the Book of Job for a graphic description of how prosperity can vanish despite our best efforts.

Living in peace is paramount, and we must not achieve wealth through crooked means. Nevertheless, economic prosperity is a positive aspect of human flourishing and, when coupled with righteousness, can be an important aspect of the goodness of creation. The Bible accordingly honors the skill and talent needed to create material prosperity. We see this in the reference to the skill and talent Bezalel and his associates brought to the building of the temple (Exodus 31:1–6) and throughout Proverbs (e.g., Proverbs 31:10-31).

Industriousness is important (Proverbs 6:6-11,13:4, Psalm 90:17), but so is the concept of the Sabbath and rest; there seems to be a rhythm of work and rest in the Bible. At the end of the first creation story, on the seventh day, God rests and makes the day holy (Genesis 2:2-3). In Exodus, God, through Moses, instructs the people to observe the seventh day as a day of rest themselves, along with aliens, their slaves, and the animals (Exodus 16:23–30, 20:8–11, 23:12, 34:21).

Over time, the Sabbath came to represent more a collection of rules than a gift. In some settings, the penalty for violating the Sabbath rules was said to be death (Exodus 31:14, Numbers 15:32-36). But Jesus changed this. Skipping ahead to the New Testament, Jesus justified plucking grain on the Sabbath by pointing out that the Sabbath was made for humankind, not the other way around (Mark 2:23-28). It is a gift to humanity, a day of rest and refreshment, and a day to enjoy creation and remember who we are in relation to God.

The Moral Foundation of Shalom

Work is important and makes an essential contribution to shalom. But our work must be conducted in an ethical manner and in a way that contributes to human well-being. The Bible provides rules that apply to work and that contribute to a productive working environment.

When he is nearing death, Moses, the lawgiver, gives people a choice between life and prosperity or death and adversity, based on their willingness to follow the divinely inspired laws he has promulgated (Deuteronomy 30:8-20).

The various rules, commandments, and statutes serve multiple purposes. Some are cultic in nature in that they are designed to reinforce loyalty to their God and maintain the religious distinction between the Israelites and competing religions. Some deal with food, purity, and health. And during war, following the rules is intended to secure God's support when going into battle.

But the law is also intended to support economic well-being and to provide guidelines for our work lives. If the people follow the rules, then the material blessings listed above are more likely to be available. If the people do not follow the rules, then the blessings will be lost, and work will be unproductive (Leviticus 26:14–20). Here complacency, especially following prosperity, is dangerous (Deuteronomy 8:11–20). The choice is between life and well-being versus death and adversity (Joshua 23:14–16).

Some of the more prominent commandments in the Bible, including six of the Ten Commandments, address the underpinnings of social cohesion. These include honoring one's father and mother (note that the household was the main economic unit) and condemning murder, adultery, theft, false witness, and coveting another's spouse or property (Exodus 20:12–17).

Social cohesion is, of course, highly important for commercial success. People need to be able to work together and trade within commonly understood, even if imperfect, ethical limits. The right to the fruit of one's labor is obvious.[99] Various forms of theft are prohibited, among them moving boundary markers (Deuteronomy 19:14), using false weights and measures (Leviticus 19:35-36, Deuteronomy 25:13-16), and bribing witnesses and judicial bodies (Exodus 23:1–3, 6–8; Deuteronomy 16:18–20). These destroy the value of work and the incentives to do honest labor.

175

Some of the laws deal with resolving disputes. If a person dishonestly takes another person's property, they are required to return the property plus 20 percent (Leviticus 6:1-5). There are also a whole host of regulations pertaining to more complicated issues such as the penalties for harming slaves, damaging an owner's animals, and others. These are often dealt with primarily in terms of commercial value (Exodus 21:18-22:14).

Personal integrity is often considered in light of social and commercial relationships, such as the warning against false witness. But there is another element to this in the Bible that merits attention. Integrity is essential in its own right, but in the Bible we see how it can also lead to personal effectiveness. In the story of Joseph and Potiphar's wife, Joseph is falsely accused of and imprisoned for a crime that his integrity prevented him from committing. Nevertheless, because of his integrity (and his finding favor in the Lord), he continues to work with power and wisdom, and people continue to turn to him for leadership (Genesis 39:1-23).

We see examples of integrity elsewhere. Those with integrity "are like trees planted by streams of water" (Psalm 1:3). They lie down and sleep in peace (Psalm 4:8) and shall never be moved (Psalm 15:5).

People should be treated well in the workplace; we should love our neighbor (Leviticus 19:18). This is the right thing to do, whether it helps our work or not, but it also leads to better working relationships. Some commandments apply more specifically to the treatment of people in the workplace. Wages of workers should not be held over until morning (Leviticus 19:13, Deuteronomy 24:14-15). Generosity should be maintained in our working relationships (Deuteronomy 15:12-15).

People have a right to work and to support themselves through their work. Landowners were not to reap to the edges of their field, nor were they to pick the grain or grapes that had fallen to the ground. This was to allow the landless poor and the aliens to harvest food for themselves, rather than begging or starving (Leviticus 19:9-10, Leviticus 23:22, Deuteronomy 24:19–21, Ruth 2:2–3).[100]

In an early agricultural economy, one bad crop year could force a family into poverty and require them to borrow against their land to avoid starvation. It would be patently unfair to require them to pledge their land or pay exorbitant interest, thereby risking their land and consequently their ability to work to provide for themselves. This is the context for the laws against taking land and other sources of income as a loan pledge and against charging interest (Deuteronomy 24:6, Nehemiah 5:1-5). It was also behind the concept of family land return, whether at the Jubilee or at other times (Leviticus 25:13-17, 23-24).

Our contemporary culture is much different, but the underlying point is nevertheless valid: people should have the opportunity to work to support themselves. Therefore businesses that provide jobs are performing a valuable service.

Falling Away

There came a time when these rules were no longer followed, at least to the extent that they should have been. Corruption set in and the people suffered. We see this especially in the Prophets, but also elsewhere in the Bible.

The story of Cain (Genesis 4:1-16) provides an exceptionally vivid account of sin in the workplace (Cain and Abel were brothers and coworkers) and the consequences of letting our hateful emotions get the best of us. In this case, acting on his resentment of his brother led Cain to kill Abel and to suffer estrangement from God, human society, and the goodness of creation.

The story of David and Bathsheba (2 Samuel 11:1-12:15) shows how sin's consequences become much worse as we try to cover up an initial sin, rather than confessing and trying to make amends.

Much of the corruption seems to have involved the rulers and their cronies, as Samuel had warned (1 Samuel 8:11-18). Beginning at least by the end of Solomon's reign, much of the wealth from trade was hoarded in the royal treasury (1 Kings 10:14-22) while the people suffered from the burdens placed on them (1 Kings 12:4). The people were not enjoying the fruits of their labor to the extent envisioned in the Torah.

A particularly striking example is the story of Naboth. Naboth owned a garden (presumably a small farm) that King Ahab desired. Naboth was unwilling to sell to Ahab, and so Ahab's wife, Jezebel, arranged for Naboth to be falsely accused of a crime and executed (1 Kings 21:1-16).

Ezekiel said that the officials became ravenous for the goods of others (Ezekiel 22:23–25), and the shepherds (leaders) fed and provided for themselves but did not meet their responsibilities to their sheep (Ezekiel 34:2–6).

The leaders oppressed the workers and the poor (Jeremiah 5:27-28). In at least some cases, this sounds like a lack of charity for the needy (Isaiah 58:6-9), but in other cases, it sounds like more aggressive acts of work-related oppression. The evil ones (presumably people with political power) schemed to take away the property of householders (Micah 2:1–2), perhaps not unlike the story of Ahab and Naboth. The poor were taxed with levies of grain (Amos 5:11). The workers, merchants, and poor were not allowed to benefit from the fruits of their work.

Corruption seems to have run through much of society. The theft of property had become rampant. Princes were accused of moving boundary markers (Hosea 5:10), officials were bribed (Amos 5:12), judicial proceedings were corrupted (Jeremiah 5:27-28), and dishonest weights and measures were used (Amos 8:4–6, Micah 6:11). Jeremiah said that "everyone is greedy for unjust gain" (Jeremiah 8:10). Dishonesty appears to have been common (Jeremiah 8:5-6, 9:1–6), and work had become unproductive as the rewards for honest labor were stolen.

The sin and corruption weakened society to the point where the nation fell to Babylonian invaders, and a great many people were forced into exile. When they were finally released, they faced the task of rebuilding their civilization (see, for example, Isaiah 61:1-4 and the books of Ezra and Nehemiah).

Wisdom in Work

In much of the preceding, we can take references to the law as guidance for society as a whole. The Bible also has a lot to say about human flourishing at the individual or family level. It is not that individual interest overrides society's interest, but rather that a flourishing society is made up of flourishing individuals and families.

Along these lines, the book of Proverbs offers insights and examples of wisdom at work. The book offers practical advice combined with a profound sense of connection with God. The practical wisdom reflects the knowledge of daily life, but the awe of God is the starting point (Proverbs

1:7, 9:10). Experiencing this awe, and letting it drive our attitude toward our life and work, is the basis of wisdom; this is what is meant by the claim that the fear of the Lord is the beginning of wisdom.

Some of the advice Proverbs offers echoes the ethical themes that run through the rest of the Bible. These include the condemnation of various forms of cheating, such as fake weights (Proverbs 20:23), treachery (Proverbs 11:3), dishonesty (Proverbs 6:19), moving property lines (Proverbs 22:28), and perverting justice for the sake of bribes (Proverbs 17:23). Personal generosity to the poor is important (Proverbs 11:24–26, 14:21, 21:13, 28:27, 31:20); moreover, special condemnation is reserved for those individuals who oppress the poor (Proverbs 14:31, 22:8–9, 22:16, 22:22–23, 28:8). In general, the virtues and behaviors that encourage social cohesion are rewarded: speaking with kindness and not in anger (Proverbs 15:1, 15:18, 16:32, 19:11, 31:26), avoiding gossip (Proverbs 11:13, 16:27–28, 18:6–8, 20:19, 26:20–21), and not belittling others (Proverbs 11:12). These rules contribute to individual well-being and a healthy work environment as well as to social cohesion.

Industriousness is held up as an essential virtue. It lets us support our families properly (Proverbs 31:21). The industrious person rises early (Proverbs 31:15), makes good plans (Proverbs 21:5), and prepares the field before building their house (Proverbs 24:27). This is contrasted with idleness. Slackness causes poverty (Proverbs 10:4–5, 13:4), and one who is slack is similar to a vandal (Proverbs 18:9). Closely related to this is the virtue of prudence; one should be wise and not devour resources foolishly (Proverbs 21:17, 20).

Business acumen, presumably developed over time, is valued (Proverbs 31:14, 16, 18, 24). To this end, wise counsel is to be sought (Proverbs 15:22, 20:18). The wise person avoids pride (Proverbs 21:4), which leads to destruction (Proverbs 16:18) and humiliation (Proverbs 29:23).

The Work-Related Teachings of Jesus and the New Testament

In this section, we will explore how the themes of the good news proclaimed by Jesus might connect with our work life. These themes apply to all of life, but they also have particular applicability to the workplace.

At the center of Jesus's message were the two great commandments. Matthew expresses them like this:

> *When the Pharisees heard that he had silenced the*
> *Sadducees, they gathered together, and one of them,*
> *a lawyer, asked him a question to test him. "Teacher,*
> *which commandment in the law is the greatest?" He*
> *said to him, "'You shall love the Lord your God with all*
> *your heart, and with all your soul, and with all your*
> *mind.' This is the greatest and first commandment.*
> *And a second is like it: 'You shall love your neighbor as*
> *yourself.' On these two commandments hang all the law*
> *and the prophets."*
>
> *Matthew 22:34-40*

This passage suggests a two-fold movement: we turn toward God and hope to do his will as we understand it, and we turn toward our fellow humans and contribute to their well-being. Jesus suggests that these are closely connected. We can apply this guidance to our work lives.

Jesus used many workplace examples and expressions that grew out of his prior experience; these reflect an understanding of and respect for daily work.[101] Examples include: the sowing of seed (Matthew 13:3–9, 13:24–30, Mark 4:26–29, 4:30–32), baking with yeast (Matthew 13:33), a merchant dealing in pearls (Matthew 13:45–46), fishing with a net (Matthew 13:47–50, Mark 1:16–20, Luke 5:1–8), a landlord hiring workers for his vineyard (Matthew 20:1–16), builders who work in stone (Matthew 21:42–44), the builder of a vineyard (Matthew 21:33–41), a diligent slave with supervisory responsibilities (Matthew 24:45–51), an investor (Matthew 25:14–30), putting new wine in new wineskins (Mark 2:21–22), the need for laborers at harvest time (Matthew 9:37–38, John 4:35–38), using a yoke (Matthew 11:28–30), fruit trees that do not bear good fruit (Mark 11:12–14), building a foundation on rock (Luke 6:46–49), a good tree that produces good fruit (Luke 6:43–45), a good shepherd (John 10:11), and pruning the branches of a vine so it will bear more fruit (John 15:1–2).

In some cases, Jesus's teachings apply explicitly to work, though these teachings can usually be taken to apply to life as a whole. The worker deserves his food (Matthew 10:10). We are to invest and make use of our talents (Matthew 25:14–30). A Samaritan cares for an injured traveler, presumably taking time away from his own work (Luke 10:25–37). People are called to follow Jesus while in the workplace, specifically while fishing (Mark 1:16–20) and tax collecting (Mark 2:13–14).

The Apostle Paul called for industriousness, as opposed to idleness. Paul worked to support himself rather than placing a burden on others (1 Thessalonians 2:9). He advised the churches with whom he was involved that each person must carry their own load (Galatians 6:5). Thieves must give up stealing so that they can work productively and share with the needy (Ephesians 4:28). People should put themselves fully into whatever task they are doing (Colossians 3:23). The people who do not support their families deny their faith (1 Timothy 5:8). Idlers should be admonished (1 Thessalonians 5:14).

Once again, we need to point out that while work is valued, it should not be idolized; love of money is, after all, a root of evil and a possible temptation (1 Timothy 6:10). A fool stores up treasure on earth and not in heaven (Luke 12:15 – 21). We should set our hopes on God, not riches (1 Timothy 6:17).

The broader teachings of Jesus also have important applicability in the workplace. To "love our neighbor as ourselves" (Mark 12:31) addresses our relationships with other people, and these relationships are highly important in our work; it is often through our work that we serve others. As discussed in the section above, we should treat people well and work at building community, whether this helps us in our work or not. Jesus has a lot to say about this, both in the Gospels and through his apostles (especially Paul).

We are to be kind and generous (Galatians 6:2, Ephesians 4:1–3, 1 John 3:11), honest and trustworthy (Matthew 5:37), act with humility and childlike openness (Luke18:14, 15-17, Romans 12:3, Philippians 2:3, 1 Peter 5:5–6), be patient (Romans 12:12, James 5:7-8)), and forgiving (Matthew 6:12, 14-15, Mark 11:25, 2 Corinthians 2:5-8). We are not to slander or speak evilly (Ephesians 4:29, James 4:11). When we have an interpersonal conflict, we are to reconcile with others (Matthew 5:23–26). We are not to judge or be hypocritical (Matthew 7:1–5). And we are to adopt what today would be called an attitude of servant leadership, whether we are in a position of formal leadership or not, and we should be focused on serving others in our work (Mark 9:33-37, Luke 22:24–27).

These virtues will contribute to the well-being of others (and our own peace of mind), contribute to a healthier working environment, and provide the basis for more productive, collaborative working relationships. They will also lead us to provide better goods and services.

We are also to love God with our entire being; this is the first of the two greatest commandments (Mark 12:28-31). We can see this as a matter of obedience, but we can also see it as turning toward God, opening ourselves to experience his presence, and trying to let God work through us. Turning toward God in prayer and other practices can help us work with a greater sense of mission, strength, and wisdom. It can help us deal with problems more calmly and behave compassionately toward others.

We see this in the life of Jesus, who frequently went off to pray by himself, apparently for renewal. And we see specific cases where turning toward God affected Jesus's work profoundly. The powerful experience of God's presence and love following his baptism drove his ministry and led him to proclaim the good news that the kingdom of God is at hand (Mark 1:9-15). Early in his ministry, he went off to pray by himself at night and emerged with a decision to extend his ministry to other cities (Mark 1:35–39). At another time, he prayed all night, and when the morning came, he worked with extraordinary decisiveness and power (Luke 6:12-19). In the garden of Gethsemane, his prayer experience gave him the courage to face death (Mark 14:32-42).

There are obvious lessons here for our own work lives. Our connection with God can be a source of purpose, wisdom, and strength, as it was for Jesus. Through prayer and other practices, we can hope that our character will be transformed, which is important for work; as Jesus put it, we will know the tree by its fruit, and the heart by the mouth (Matthew 12:33-37, Luke 6:43–45).

There can be a tendency in some quarters to see the New Testament, and the gospel, as giving less weight to materiality and physical embodiment than the Old Testament does. Indeed, the emphasis changes somewhat in the New Testament, but there is still a strong element of materiality. For example, we see Jesus feeding the people real food (Mark 8:1-9), providing wine at a wedding at Cana (John 2:1-11), and healing physical ailments, including deafness, blindness, and leprosy (Matthew 15:30-31, Luke 7:21-23).

We can also see the materiality expressed in the various ways that the end of time is described. Despite their differences, they all point to a degree of materiality and embodiment. The most vivid example is in the book of Revelation. The vision of John of Patmos points to a new city, a new Jerusalem, coming down from the heavens in glorious material splendor, with walls, jewels, precious metals, and other forms of strikingly beautiful materiality (Revelation 21:10-21). John's vision includes the various peoples of the earth bringing and contributing the material product of their work and culture (Revelation 21:24-26).

The Apostle Paul expected the sound of God's trumpet at the end, Jesus physically descending from heaven, and people who had died rising out of the ground, presumably with new bodies of some sort (1 Thessalonians 4:16-17).

In at least some cases, Jesus seems to have spoken of an immediate postmortem entry into an afterworld. In the story of Lazarus and the rich man, the materiality was such that physical thirst was possible (Luke 16:19-31). In the Gospel According to John, Jesus speaks of there being many dwelling places for his disciples (John 14:1-3). And on the cross, he told the man next to him that they would be in paradise that very day (Luke 23:43).

Each of these examples provides a different image, but each also seems to reflect a desire to maintain a degree of materiality.

There is a similar pattern in the post-resurrection appearances. The empty tomb points to materiality of sorts; the thinking seems to be that if God raises Jesus, then this must involve his body which could not, therefore, have remained in the tomb. The post-resurrection appearances themselves are all quite mysterious; it is not always clear what is actually going on. The resurrected Jesus behaves in ways that do not seem to be consistent with a physical embodiment, such as not being recognized on the road to Emmaus (Luke 24:13-16), suddenly appearing amidst the disciples (Luke 24:36, John 20:19), vanishing (Luke 24:31), and being lifted into heaven (Luke 24:51). But despite the mystery and ambiguity, the tradition took pains to make the materiality clear. Jesus broke bread (Luke 24:30), ate fish (Luke 24:42-43), prepared breakfast (John 21:12), had touchable wounds (Luke 24:39-40, John 20:20, 27), and physically walked to Emmaus (Luke 24:13-29). The Gospel writers meant to convey materiality.

In combination, these passages seem to suggest that we live in a material world, as embodied beings, but our spiritual connection with God and divine reality is nevertheless of primary importance. And this applies to our work. Our work in the material world is essential but must not be idolized. Our relationship with God and with transcendent reality endures despite setbacks and even devastation. Our work is important; we should keep it in a proper perspective and understand its connection to shalom and divine reality.

Appendix B

Work in the Twenty-First Century

There is no doubt that work has been changing quite rapidly for a large number of people. Obvious causes have included rapid technological development, changes in global markets, pandemics, economic setbacks, and social/political trends. At the time of this writing, more people are becoming conscious of economic security issues and personal safety, more inclined to work and meet remotely when they can, and more interested in the quality of their work life. We are finding new ways to work; for some, this means working remotely, for others, it might mean other adjustments.

In some ways, much of the more recent change represents an acceleration of longer-term trends. Prior to the pandemic, technology and culture were creating new ways of looking at and going about business and our work. Remote working was becoming more accepted in some quarters, though nothing like it is now. Communication over the internet had become hugely more efficient (even if often less personal). And there was a long-term trend toward greater individual agency and initiative, driven to a large extent by technological developments that put more productive power and scale in the hands of individuals.

The rate of change accelerated during the pandemic. Technology has played a key role, but much of this technology (such as video conferencing) was already available; the biggest factor seems to have been rapid innovation by businesses and individuals in the face of new challenges, and a corresponding rapid increase in the adoption rate of technology and new ways of doing things. People and businesses became more adaptive.

In this appendix, I will focus on what I believe are longer-term trends in our work lives. While the recent health and economic crises have accelerated these trends, for the most part the trends predate the crises and will, I believe, be with us for a long time afterward. There are three topics upon which I would like to focus:

1. Personal agency and initiative

2. Remote work and the need to build community in new ways

3. Alienation from work and the challenge of rapid change

Each of these reflects the effects of rapid technological and cultural change.

I offer two caveats. First, none of us can see into the future; the most we can do is identify trends that we think might influence it so that we can begin to prepare ourselves. Second, we need to be wary of generalizations; circumstances and attitudes vary greatly among individuals and situations and I certainly do not want to suggest that we are all going through the same challenges and experiences.

Personal Agency and Initiative

The changing nature of personal agency in our work lives is one of the most important long-term trends of contemporary work, though it does not get a great deal of publicity. By personal agency, I mean the degree to which individuals can act on their own volition, be responsible for their decisions, and have an effect of their choosing. I believe that personal agency is an essential contributor to one's psychological and spiritual growth and needs to be protected and expanded whenever possible.

In many cases, the advancing technologies have placed greater power and productivity in the hands of individuals and, at the same time, has increased the need for companies to give more decision-making authority to the people doing the work. People can do more and develop results on a larger scale, even if they are working remotely. They also have access to more information and can communicate, even globally, very quickly. This has facilitated the increase we have seen in people working from home and has made many companies more responsive to a changing business environment.

As a result, over several decades there has been a shift toward jobs that are more interesting and challenging, and less boring. This reduction in boredom applies more or less equally to office jobs, manufacturing jobs, and work from home. When I took my first corporate job in 1973, office workers in medium to large companies were often situated in large rooms with row upon row of desks at which people performed the most mundane work imaginable. An example might be the accounts payable clerk who would spend each day matching paper purchase orders with the corresponding receiving documents and invoices, stapling them together, and stamping them as approved for payment. There were many people who spent their entire day doing this type of work, living primarily for coffee breaks, lunch breaks, weekends, and retirement.

In the case of factory workers, a typical job might have been somewhat more physical but still highly mundane and repetitive. I knew of cases where a person spent all day performing one simple task such as stamping out a metal part and then passing it on to the next station. Some of these jobs still exist, but machines have replaced many of them. In the short-term, this created hardships that we should not gloss over, but in the long-term, it has made the work of many people much more interesting to the extent that they are able to bring more intelligence and initiative to the work at hand.

A corollary to this is that during prosperous times, a significant proportion of employees and job seekers are looking for interesting and fulfilling work; employers with jobs that offer such potential are more likely to attract engaged and interested workers. Having an engaged workforce is a critical advantage in many more industries than in the past.

The broader availability of technical and other information has also been a significant factor. Today people in many situations can find the necessary information for their work and professional growth using online resources, much of it for free. We can attend webinars, take open online classes, and download books and articles. We can find education for almost any kind of work cheaply and quickly. We may soon see a time when employers place more importance on education and professional development obtained apart from degreed programs than they do on the credentials represented by a degree.

Thomas Friedman explores the subject of open education in his book, *Thank You for Being Late: An Optimist's Guide to Thriving in an Age of Accelerations*. He spends time exploring the work of Sal Kahn and the Kahn Institute. Kahn's mission is to make education free and accessible to everyone; he and others seem to be succeeding.[102]

As Friedman, Kahn, and others point out, while education is now easily available, people need to take ownership of their own education; they need to act as agents in planning and pursuing their own development.[103] The days of following a well-marked path or waiting for one's employer to take the initiative are ending. Here, too, we see the importance of individual initiative and agency, and especially the need for individuals to respond and take responsibility for their own development.

While I see the opportunity for individual agency as highly positive, not everyone agrees; some would rather not have more personal agency and freedom in their work life. And, of course, in a difficult economic time, people are more inclined to opt for financial security.

I once had a conversation with a German aerospace scientist. She had worked for several years before the fall of the Berlin wall for a scientific institute of the East German government. To my surprise, she was not happy about the fall of the wall and the liberation of the eastern bloc. Especially striking was the attitude of her father who, as she relayed it, had spent most of his life working under communism (I do not remember his occupation, but it was not a high-status job like that of his daughter). I would have thought he would have been happy to be free of the communists, but in fact, he hated the ending of the dictatorship. In his view, life under communism was psychologically easier; he just showed up for work and got paid. He did not have to make any decisions about what type of work he wanted to do, and that had been the way he liked it. Now he experienced anxiety as he made decisions for himself.

I tend to assume that increasing personal agency is positive, but that is not the case for all people, especially when there is heightened concern for economic security. I wish this were not the case because I believe that personal agency is essential for personal and maybe spiritual growth.

We should also note that there are problems that can work against our sense of agency, if we let them.

An example might be the problem of busyness. People often complain of having too much to do in too little time. You might be in this situation yourself; people, in general, do indeed seem to be busier than in the past. It is not always clear whether this is due to the pressures of work or more demanding time commitments outside of work, but it is clear that certain occupational/demographic groups are especially burdened. These include single working parents and dual-career parents of young children. Early and mid-career professionals, especially if they are ambitious, can also be highly busy. And some people need to work very long hours at low pay to stay afloat.

Health care workers during public health crises can be especially busy, to the point that their health might be at risk.

Some people also confront the "24/7" always-on syndrome. This is where one is always available by cell phone and email. This can reduce or even eliminate the opportunity to leave work behind and find time away for recharging and for enjoying leisure activities.

There have recently been several examples of people experimenting with ways to temporarily limit their involvement in work by switching off their email and phones during particular periods, communicating to coworkers the hours when they are or are not available, and doing a better job of filtering communications. These steps can be helpful.

On the other hand, some of us really do need to be available around the clock. For example, before I left the food industry in 2018, I was the owner of the company and, by necessity, was involved in food and transportation safety. I needed to be available and could not delegate the safety-related decision-making responsibility to somebody else. As a result, I kept my cell phone handy, and I usually checked emails and text messages several times in the evening and on holidays. And to be honest, I felt something of a compulsion to check for messages even beyond the safety requirements.

There are also distractions. Most of us are probably familiar with the temptation to check news sites or social media platforms more frequently than necessary or useful. We know the experience of being drawn into significant time wasters, maybe in the form of deliberate clickbait. There are well-funded marketers and researchers who work very hard to keep us distracted.

A significant reason why social media platforms foster so much divisiveness is that their algorithms are designed to promote engagement and this usually means promoting the most controversial and divisive tweets and posts. Whether we are talking about divisive political posts or other forms of clickbait, there is certainly a lot of work and research being put into tempting us to waste our time for the sake of advertising revenue.

There is one other area of concern regarding our sense of agency—the rapid expansion of what some people call surveillance capitalism along with the oversight of citizens by government agencies. A significant portion of the innovation in digital technology has been devoted to newer, more insidious and dishonest ways of gathering personal information through our digital activity and through things like facial recognition software. Tech giants have also found sneaky ways to track our location through our cell phones, even when they are not in use (by us).

We are beginning to see the use of these capabilities by dictatorships; there is also the possibility of intrusive tracking being used in the workplace, thereby making it a more restrictive, less creative, and perhaps demoralizing environment. We may soon see employers, and schools, with the capability to monitor where their employees or students spend their time. We will undoubtedly see countervailing developments designed to block this spying, but we still need to acknowledge the problem and be prepared.

Each of these threats can suppress our sense of agency. There is a paradox, however. In each case, a large part of the solution might be to strengthen our sense of agency in response. We have it within our power to cut out the distractions, get control over unnecessary busyness, and remake our digital interactions in a way that is more positive and life-giving.

———

Work that calls for a deeper sense of personal agency also calls for a deeper faith or spirituality.

For one thing, if we are to operate with more responsibility for our actions, we need to have a clear framework for making decisions. Having clear ethical principles is an obvious example. A person who makes decisions somewhat independently is going to need a stronger sense of ethics than someone who sees themselves as a mere cog without influence.

If we are going to play a greater role in charting our own course, we need a clear sense of our purpose and the meaning of our work; we need to know who we are and what we are trying to accomplish. This is especially true in times or situations of uncertainty and change.

We also need to be stronger individuals, and this requires character strengths such as self-regulation, courage, and patience, as we explored earlier.

I would guess that when we feel responsible for charting our own course, the great existential questions are more likely to come to the surface. These existential questions involve the mystery of our existence—questions like, Why am I here? What is my purpose? Does my identity die with my biological body? Does my life have value and validity? Ultimately how we engage the great mystery, and live into it, has a lot to do with how we experience and act upon our sense of agency.

All of this requires a strong spiritual foundation.

Remote Work and the Need to Build Community in New Ways

Personal relationships are essential in most of our work lives. By personal relationships, I mean relationships between people, not relationships that are deemed personal because they are outside the workplace.

It is clear that personal relationships have a lot to do with the meaning and value we find in our work. Work is more fulfilling and enjoyable when we have good relations with the people with whom we work. It can also be a source of satisfaction to know the people for whom our work provides value. And as a practical matter, our work is likely to be far more effective if we have strong collaborative relationships with the people with whom we work, whether coworkers, suppliers, affiliated companies, or customers.

The reverse is true, as well. Weak or even antagonistic interpersonal relationships can significantly inhibit the sense of meaning and purpose we find in our work.

Even before the pandemic, the new communication tools significantly expanded our ability to work with large numbers of people. Email and various messaging platforms enable us to convey information much more quickly, and this applies especially to global communications. And various software platforms allow us to speak in real time, often on video, with people in multiple locations, cheaply and without being constrained by distance. And we no longer need to be in an office to do so.

We are all familiar with how the newer video communication tools have greatly expanded many people's ability to work remotely and have made a huge change in their working environment. This trend accelerated exponentially with the pandemic; even after it, the incidence of working from home (and the related hybrid arrangements) continues to be higher than it was before, though not as high as during the lockdowns. This will continue to vary by type of work and industry.

The trend toward working at home has also generated huge efficiencies by reducing commute and travel time and possibly by reducing investment in central offices. While some of this seems to be offset by people spending more time in video conferences, the work will undoubtedly become more efficient with more experience.

While I consider all of this to be a big step forward, there is a potential downside: if we are not careful, some of the tools—especially text-based digital tools, but also video conferencing tools—can inhibit the forming of more personal working relationships. This is especially true of people who work remotely, but also applies to the relationships of people who work in the same building but do most of their communicating electronically.

Text-based digital tools encourage us to send task-related information very quickly and efficiently. Simple requests for information and the corresponding responses can, in some cases, take well less than a minute. This is far more efficient than a video chat, telephone call, or letter, the first two of which usually involve at least some polite chatter that is extraneous to the actual request or response. In my last food industry position, if I had to perform the same communications but without email or text messaging, it would probably have taken me two or three times longer to do my work.

While efficient, text-based tools often do a very poor job of facilitating personal relationships. In-person conversations convey to us much more about the people with whom we are speaking. We can see their emotional reactions and pick up visual and subconscious cues about their personalities and maybe their orientation toward work and life, at least in the broad sense. We can develop an understanding of how optimistic or pessimistic they are, whether they like their work, how they react to other people in the room, etc. It also makes it more natural for us to learn about each other's lives and interests outside of work.

Video meetings can be much better than text-based communications for developing interpersonal relationships, but even here things like eye contact tend to be minimized. For most of us, they are not as effective as in-person conversations. We can pick up some of the nuances and visual cues, but not all of them. We can also pick up a more accurate sense of a person's engagement and interest level when speaking in person.

Video meetings have become widely used. There is no question in my mind that they are a big step forward in terms of efficiency, especially when we take into account the reduction in people traveling long distances to attend meetings and conferences. But I suspect we will also see a decline in collaborative creativity as we have fewer serendipitous encounters. Some network theorists have suggested that the information and insights on which creativity and innovation often rely are encouraged by "weak connections" that tend to spread information and ideas faster and farther. These weak connections are often unplanned—meeting someone from another department by chance in the hallway or cafeteria, an introduction at a conference social event; these are things that are unlikely to happen on a video call.

We must continue to take advantage of digital technologies; I would not want to go back to the old ways. But we also need to recognize the potential obstacle to the development of community and intentionally work to offset this problem. Remote workers should be brought into a central office periodically and encouraged to engage with their coworkers. Telephone and video conferencing should be used as an intermediate step between face-to-face meetings and text messages or emails to help bridge the gap. We can develop the art of making some of our emails a bit more personal (but let's not go overboard!). We can be alert to opportunities to provide individual support for our coworkers and others, even if from a distance. And we can develop the skills and techniques needed to develop rapport and interpersonal connections at a distance.

There are indications that leaders who are transparent, open, and empathetic find it easier to develop collaboration in online environments. In some cases, team leaders open video meetings with five minutes spent checking with the participants in regard to personal issues; this allows people an opportunity to alert the group to problems they are having that they would not ordinarily interject into an online business conversation.

Our faith or spirituality can play a crucial role by helping us remember that each person has dignity and value, even apart from our value in the workplace, and therefore deserves respect. Adopting this attitude and letting it influence our interactions are bound to make our communications and our relationships more humane.

Alienation from Work and the Challenge of Rapid Change

We sometimes hear commentators, including theologians, talk about how the contemporary work environment is alienating; by this, they mean people are bored, lack a sense of purpose, and might even feel at odds with their work. Different reasons are given for this; these can include the fact that many of us no longer see the end product our work produces, many of our organizations are too large to foster a sense of personal connection, working remotely makes some people feel disconnected, there is too much internal competition and backstabbing within our organizations, or some work is sheer drudgery. Sometimes the commentators provide anecdotes or the results of selected studies to prove the point.

Those of us who have spent time working in a variety of different environments, however, usually realize that many of these points are overly broad generalizations. There is undoubtedly some truth to all of them, but I do not believe any of these observations are so generally true as to guide us in all or even most cases. There is a huge variety of working environments and a huge variety in how people respond to these environments.

The presence of alienation is not necessarily determined by the worker's economic or social status. I have seen people working in tough jobs that many observers would characterize as drudgery but they nevertheless work in an engaged and purposeful manner. They might rather be doing something else, but it would be unfair to describe them as alienated.

On the other hand, I have seen people in high status or so-called glamorous jobs who find their work quite boring. The status of the work is not a reliable indicator of how engaged particular individuals will be.

While the attitude and interpretation of the group is important, in many cases it is the individual who plays the most significant role in defining the meaning of the work that they are doing. There are people in almost any given cohort who find important purpose in their work, while others, doing essentially the same job in the same social setting, do not. Some people seem to find it easier to find meaning and a sense of purpose in their work, no matter what the circumstances.

The fit among the person, the social situation, and the work can significantly affect people's ability to find meaning and purpose in what they are doing, as can their understanding of how their work contributes to the greater good and the well-being of others.

This sense of meaning can apply either to the job or to the task. It can also apply to their membership in the organization; if they believe the organization of which they are a part is making a worthwhile contribution to society, their work in support of that organization will be more meaningful.

There are other factors. People are more likely to work with purpose if they believe that they are using their particular talents constructively; if they believe they are respected and appreciated by the people with whom and for whom they work; and if they believe they are growing and advancing.

The rapidity with which one's work environment changes can be a critical factor. The ideal job would, among other things, integrate two types of considerations. First, it would be designed to produce high value in accord with the purpose of the organization. Second, it would have a high degree of fit with the people doing the work—their values, aspirations, desire for purpose, and the factors we discussed earlier such as the need for relationship, competency, and autonomy/agency.

These task-related and human-related considerations are not necessarily in conflict. People take satisfaction from being productive, and productivity is likely to be higher if there is a good fit between the person and the task.

But they can get out of balance. Organizations can overemphasize short-term productivity while neglecting the human side; over time, such work is likely to become less productive as people feel increasingly disengaged from it. On the other hand, some organizations and leaders can emphasize human feelings and desires and lose sight of the importance of productivity. Neither is likely to be successful relative to competition over the long-term.

The relationship between these is dynamic rather than static as changes ripple through society and organizations. A system that had been balanced can become unbalanced; as the environment changes, continual attention and effort are needed to move the balance closer to an equilibrium point. An effective leader helps people continue to restore the balance.

———

The times in which we live require us to deal with an extraordinary level of change as well as the likelihood of crisis. The material in the main chapters of this book provide much of the content that would be applicable here. We need to develop character strengths such as courage, resilience, persistence, humility, hope, and compassion. We need to remember who we are and be mindful of the dignity of all people. We should be inspired by our opportunity to work toward a better world in the form of shalom and human flourishing. We need to resist the sins that tend to grow from stress. And spiritual practices can help us stay grounded.

Most importantly, we need to continue to participate in the sacred by turning toward God and then turning toward the world and working to make things better.

Appendix C

Spirituality and the State of Flow

If you have experienced a state of flow, you probably remember it as an enjoyable experience. It is usually associated with heightened concentration, deeper awareness, and maybe greater effectiveness, and is sometimes thought of as being "in the zone." Most of us would probably like to spend more time in flow, whether in leisure activities or at work.

The state of flow is considered a positive psychological condition and has been researched primarily from a nonreligious point of view, and appropriately so. But I believe there can also be a religious or spiritual dimension to this experience. Being aware of flow and this other dimension can deepen the meaning we find in our work, intensify our experience, and help us move more easily toward this beneficial state.

The Concept of Flow

Psychologist Mihaly Csikszentmihalyi was the first to identify, study, and name the experience of flow, describing it as an optimal experience in which:

> Concentration is so intense that there is no attention
> left over to think about anything irrelevant, or to worry
> about problems. Self-consciousness disappears, and
> the sense of time becomes distorted. An activity that
> produces such experiences is so gratifying that people
> are willing to do it for its own sake, with little concern

for what they will get out of it, even when it is difficult, or dangerous.[104]

When we are in a state of flow, we are fully engaged with the task, to the point that awareness and action seem to merge. We feel highly effective and in control. No attention is available for distractions such as concerns about job security or status. Not coincidentally, we often experience a feeling of enjoyment.[105]

How do we reach this flow state? Csikszentmihalyi suggests several factors that can contribute, among them:

1. We can give our full attention to the task. As we do so, our self-concern disappears.

2. There is a good fit between the task's challenges and our skills, with enough challenge to require our full attention and allow for a sense of growth, but not so much difficulty that we become frustrated or overwhelmed.

3. We believe there is a good chance that we can successfully complete the task.

4. The task has clear goals and feedback that provide a structure and a basis for knowing whether we are progressing as we work.

5. We feel we are able to exert some control over our work.[106]

I am reminded of the earlier comments about Vallerand's harmonious passion and about Deci and Ryan's identification of our need to experience competence and autonomy/agency.

Entering a flow state as we work requires us to direct our attention toward the task at hand fully and completely. Sometimes this might happen naturally, but I suspect that most of us need to work at focusing our attention more effectively. Practice probably helps, I would think.

The payoff can be very beneficial. Imagine if we could spend more of our work time in a state of flow. We would be fully engaged, focused, energized, and effective, and would probably find more enjoyment and satisfaction in our work. We would also be completing our work more quickly, allowing extra time for our other activities.

Is There a Spiritual or Religious Connection?

Csikszentmihalyi spoke of flow as a psychological, not a religious, concept, at least as religion is conventionally understood. Nevertheless, I do think we can find several possible points of connection that can deepen our experience and understanding.

The biblical concept of shalom is one of them. Shalom includes a sense of peace and harmony in several dimensions—personal, social, spiritual, economic, etc. One might think of it as being in a right relationship with God, our fellow humans, our deeper self, and maybe our work. When the word "peace" appears in the New Testament (e.g., the greeting "peace be with you"), it usually refers to shalom.

In our work lives, we might think of shalom as the basis for holistic flourishing—a flourishing that incorporates each of the dimensions of human life.

When we are in a state of flow, we seem to be at peace with ourselves and our work, and I would guess with others as well. We are not beset by greed, pride, hatred, petty resentments, excessive self-concern, and the various other sins that can distract us. The virtues found in the Bible, such as patience, humility, and courage, seem to encourage this peace as does the biblical injunction to observe the Sabbath.

As the Psalmist puts it, people with integrity will "lie down and sleep in peace" (Psalm 4:8); God grants this to those who are not troubled by unwanted thoughts, which sounds like the result of an ordered consciousness to me.

Another point of connection might be Csikszentmihalyi's observation that as we become absorbed in the task, our concept of self (and, I would say, our self-concern) recedes from our consciousness and we might experience a sense of enjoyment. I suspect that this sounds at least vaguely familiar to many religious people.

When else do we experience these types of feelings? We might think of engaging in spiritual practices such as prayer, meditation, and worship;

helping and working with other people; being carried away by music; or acting on a sense of calling. The triggers and experiences might be somewhat different for different people, but I suggest a commonality. In each case, as we lose ourselves in the experience and our self-concern recedes, we might experience feelings of peace and positivity.

The New Testament frequently asks us to let go of our excessive self-concern. We see this reflected in the virtues of humility (Ephesians 4:1-3, Luke 18:14, Romans 12:3, Philippians 2:3, 1 Peter 5:6 and elsewhere). We are also asked to let go of our worries (Matthew 6:25-34, Luke 12:22-31, and 1 Peter 5:7). We are advised by Jesus that, paradoxically,

> *For those who want to save their life will lose it, and*
> *those who lose their life for my sake, and the sake of the*
> *gospel, will save it.*
>
> *Mark 8:35*

We might think of some of the virtues as potentially both precursors and expressions of an ordered consciousness.

For some of us, the state of flow might be inherently spiritual. The experience represents a state of mind that is fully engaged and fully conscious; we feel more alive and more like who we are meant to be. It depends on what one means by "spiritual," of course, but it seems to me that as we experience flow, we feel that we are moving in the right direction—we might say in the direction ordained by God.

A Point of Clarification: When I speak of our self-concern receding, this is not necessarily a collectivist or communitarian concept, nor does it mean subjecting our will to the opinions of a group. Just because our self-concern diminishes, it does not mean that our individual agency vanishes with it. To the contrary, I believe that our sense of agency and purpose might become more robust as we stop worrying about our various distractions. This is especially true if the potential distractions are driven by concerns that are extrinsic to the person or the task, such as social pressure or the desire for social status or financial security. To the degree that the state of flow allows our actions to line up with our deeper internal values and drives, the experience can be liberating and can move us away from being dominated by our social setting.

Can Spiritual Practices Help Us Enter a State of Flow?

I think they can, for the following reasons.

Spiritual practices such as prayer and meditation can help us focus on the task at hand, let go of distractions, and work in a more relaxed state. They help us concentrate, in effect reducing the disorder in our minds.

To the extent that our faith helps us develop virtues that apply in the workplace (in particular patience, humility, compassion, equanimity, and transparency), we are less likely to be burdened by the distractions of resentment, anger, fear, pride, social pressure, and excessive self-concern. We are thereby more likely to be able to engage in the task at hand with an ordered consciousness.

Knowing and accepting who we are at a deeper level might also help us eliminate the distractions; faith helps provide this.

Is Flow Always Good?

There is one further issue with which we must deal: is the state of flow always good? Can we enter a state of flow when we are in pursuit of inherently harmful goals?

On the one hand, it is hard to imagine someone being in a state of flow if they are under the control of various sins, petty or otherwise, such as greed or covetousness. And it is pretty well accepted that encouraging the traditional virtues does indeed enhance our sense of well-being and our ability to focus. One would hope that behaving with integrity in pursuit of a good cause would help us move toward a state of flow.

On the other hand, ordered consciousness and the state of flow do not appear to be dependent on the moral value of the intended outcome of our actions. At least, I do not know of any reason why they should be.

Perhaps we should leave this as an open question. In the meantime, we can protect ourselves by remembering the importance of having a robust moral framework and letting it guide our actions.

Appendix D

The Opportunity for Churches

Churches Could Serve and Engage Many More People
By Meeting Their Work-Related Spiritual Needs

Many people want to experience a deeper sense of purpose and fulfillment in their work; a work life ministry can help them achieve this. It can help them develop a deeper awareness of God as they go through their work week. It can help them develop the strength and wisdom to overcome obstacles, understand how their work contributes to the well-being of others, and build community. And it can introduce them to spiritual practices that connect them with their deeper purpose.

This is not just a church growth issue. It is an opportunity for the church to fulfill its mission in a way that can significantly affect the lives of a substantial number of people.

There are exclusively secular programs that cater to some of our professional needs; these are often based on lessons learned from actual work experience and research in various social science fields. These programs can be of considerable value, but their predominantly secular approach ignores the natural human desire to connect with something deeper than ourselves and to reflect this sense of connection in our daily lives. Without a theological or spiritual grounding, purely secular programs are less helpful than they might otherwise be.

Therefore, a church-based approach that combines practical work-related knowledge and experience with theological and spiritual reflection could meet a very large need among adults for whom work is important. A church could meet this need through a combination of sermons, specialized small groups, speaking events that address work-related issues, fellowship opportunities, pastoral and lay counseling, and other offerings.

An effective church-based ministry needs to understand the work-related spiritual needs of the people it hopes to serve. It should also reflect a reasonable understanding of the contemporary environments within which they work.

Spiritual Needs in the Workplace

People and their work vary greatly; it is critical to avoid over-generalizing. Nevertheless, here are some of the more common spiritual needs.

1. People seek a deeper sense of purpose in their work. Most people want to experience a sense of connection with something deeper or larger than themselves—for most, this means a greater awareness of God as they work. And many have a corresponding desire to contribute to the greater good and the well-being of other people. Understanding how they can express these through their work can form the basis for a deeper sense of purpose.

2. People face serious challenges in their work lives that get in the way of shalom. These come in the form of various sins, misfortunes, and adversities. Spiritual strength and insights can help them overcome these.

3. Many people are interested in prayer and other spiritual practices; a large percentage of people pray frequently. We can help them find practices that fit into the rhythm of their work and help them quickly turn their attention toward God. These practices can help them stay calm amidst stress and conflict, refocus their attention, and reconnect with their deeper purpose.

4. The virtues taught by most churches, like integrity, kindness, hope, humility, and courage, help people overcome obstacles more effectively. They also help us live better and open us to lives of spiritual depth.

5. Most of us desire professional growth; this is increasingly important in the modern workplace. While this is often seen in secular terms, professional growth can also have a spiritual dimension.

6. People form friendships and community in their work lives, but for most of us, there also comes a time when we need a community of peers apart from our work. Such a community can become a sounding board for reflection and a source of support during times of stress.

Program Options

One might start by considering the following options:

1. **Sermon Series on Faith and Work Issues:** This is a good place to start the conversation. A good sermon series will affirm the importance of work and its connection with faith and will put the discussion into the proper theological perspective. By starting the conversation publicly, the series might also bring forward people interested in discussing the topic further and who might also be willing to participate on a ministry organizing team. People should be invited from the pulpit to express their interest and to volunteer.

2. **Speaker Series on Work-Related Issues:** An effective series could include expert speakers on work-related hot button issues (stress, burnout, interpersonal conflict, work/life balance, etc.). The right expert speaking at a public event can provide very helpful insights and, if properly promoted, can attract and engage people from outside the church. For example, at the Work Life Forum events organized by the Center for Faith and Enterprise and hosted by La Cañada Presbyterian Church in California, of the 100 to 200 people in attendance at each event, roughly half have come from outside the church. Such events can also provide an opportunity

for people with similar interests to talk informally before and after the event.

3. **Work-Related Small Groups:** These provide an opportunity to build community, share common issues, and reflect on the connection between the participants' faith and work. Time can be provided for prayer, reading and engaging scripture, reflecting on the connections between scripture and work, and thinking about how to integrate our faith into our work week. Study guides can be made available.

4. **Spiritual Practices:** Spiritual practices such as prayer can play an important role, especially if they can be integrated into the rhythm of the work week in a way that honors both work and spirituality. For most people, this means practices that can be done quickly and frequently and that can become a habit. I have been involved with retreats (*Spiritual Practices for the Active Work Life*) and classes (*Spirituality for Busy People*) that explore examples of such practices. Examples of such practices are included in Chapter Six.

There are other initiatives that can also bear fruit, depending on the circumstances. Among them are:

Workplace Visitations: Matt Rusten, executive director of the Made to Flourish network, recommends that a church that is serious about faith and work integration have a pastor who visits congregants in their workplace. This helps the pastor understand workplace issues and also signals the interest of the church. When this is not practical, or against company policy, online video calls could be a substitute, though physical presence in the workplace would certainly provide the pastor with a better feel for the nature of the business.

Made to Flourish's mission is to empower "pastors and their churches to integrate faith, work, and economic wisdom for the flourishing of their communities."[107]

Industry Groups: I have not been personally involved in these, but I know of a program conducted by Caleb Monroe at Reality Church of Los Angeles. Monroe has several different industry-specific groups, some with as many as 150 people. Because of its location, Reality LA has a strong representation from the entertainment industry in its congregation and has large, active groups for writers, actors, and musicians. Young adults are heavily represented in this mix. When it is time to develop a new industry group, Monroe begins by setting up informal dinners with people in that industry to learn what the unique needs and struggles are for Christians in that field. From the dinners, he also identifies the people he believes would be the strongest leaders for the new group and invites them to help plan and organize the new offering.

Fellows Programs: These are six- to twelve-month programs that bring together a small group of highly committed Christians to study scripture and theological writings. The programs are promoted by Redeemer Presbyterian Church in New York and by The Fellows Initiative and can be found in multiple locations. The groups typically meet once per week with an occasional retreat or monthly special event. On paper, the curriculum often looks quite seminary oriented, with readings of serious theologians such as Augustine, John Calvin, Martin Luther, and Lesslie Newbigin. I think the assumption is that the texts provide classical theology, and the group discussions bring out the work life implications.

Steve Lindsey of the Center for Faith and Work/LA runs similar programs in Los Angeles. His Framework Fellows Program "equips leaders with a reimagined vision of their work's purpose and its strong relationship to the gospel's renewing power for cultural transformation of Los Angeles."[108]

Small Business Anti-Poverty Ministry: People in business are quite often attracted by the idea of helping poor, struggling entrepreneurs start and build their businesses. This can suggest an important area of church ministry that can both help the less fortunate and make clear the connection between faith and work.

Business development can be important for helping people climb out of poverty; this is true in both developed and less developed countries. The right program can provide an opportunity for people with business and other skills to meet this need and use their talents in important new ways. The right program can also highlight the importance of work in commercial enterprises as a way to contribute to shalom. For these reasons, participating in a program that helps small entrepreneurs can be an important part of a church-based faith and work program.

There are several organizations with which churches can work. The one with which I have been most involved is Partners Worldwide, based in Grand Rapids, Michigan (disclosure: I was the Chairman of the Board several years ago). Partners Worldwide not only accepts donations but also seeks volunteers who can use their work-related expertise to help small entrepreneurs. The opportunity to give not just money but also work-related talents adds an important dimension to the ministry.[109]

There are other organizations that provide loans and training to micro-entrepreneurs and to small and medium enterprises and that will accept donations from church members.

Daily Email Devotions: Several organizations publish daily email devotions. Mark Roberts of Fuller Seminary's Max De Pree Center for Leadership offers a popular one designed for leaders; he sends subscribers a Life for Leaders email each day with a Bible passage, brief reflection, and prayer. He provides the message himself on weekdays and has a team of volunteers who take turns writing for the weekends. His email devotions have a very broad reach and can be utilized by churches.[110]

Special Situations: Some circumstances suggest more specialized opportunities. Downtown churches might offer noon prayer services or music events for people who work in the area. More liturgical churches could offer special liturgies for workers, for particular occupations, or for when people face a change in their work status. Less formal churches might interview individuals about their work lives as part of the sermon.

Factors That Contribute to a Strong Ministry

Select Leaders With Workplace Experience

Theological and spiritual grounding is vital for leaders of faith and work programs, but so is significant work experience outside of church and charity environments. The ideal leader of such a program would combine both. If a leader with both qualifications is not available, then the church could pair a leader with significant outside experience with a pastor who is interested in bridging the different perspectives. A church could also set up a council to manage this process and facilitate the conversation.

One trap to avoid: in some cases, business people can be too deferential to religious professionals when it comes to matters of theology. It is important that unordained leaders be encouraged to see themselves as full participants in theological discussions and to feel free to bring their workplace perspective into the conversation.

The church should also identify one or more contact people who are available to discuss work-related issues and receive feedback from members of the congregation. This person or persons should be clearly identified, perhaps in the weekly bulletin and on the church website. This signals the church's interest and provides an easy contact point for conversations and expressions of interest, and should foster more frequent informal discussions. The contact person does not have to be a pastor or staff person; moreover, a layperson with considerable non-church work experience might be in a good position to discuss work-related issues that emerge in business settings.

Address Serious Work-Related Issues

While a church-based program should not be expected to help with technical decisions such as whether or not to buy a particular piece of equipment, many of our most painful work-related issues involve, at least indirectly, our relationships with other people, our self-identity, and our larger purpose. Specific issues can include stress, burnout, challenges to our integrity, interpersonal conflict, the role of compassion, developing purpose, building community, spiritual practices, dealing with failure, and the pursuit of opportunity. These are issues for which a church-based ministry could be quite helpful.

Discussion should go beyond theological or philosophical ideas and incorporate the work issues that participants might actually be facing. Programs that limit themselves to theological and philosophical issues are likely to be of sustainable interest only to people with high involvement in religion or the church; they are unlikely to engage people outside the church or even a majority of people within the church.

It depends on the issue, of course, but I believe that the most effective programs combine resources from both secular and religious or spiritual sources. In the case of work-related burnout, for example, I have been involved with discussions that incorporate insights from psychological research but also encourage reflection on the story of Elijah in the wilderness and the role of spiritual renewal.

Affirm the Value and Importance of Work

It is crucial to affirm the value of most of the types of work in which participants are engaged. Not all work is good, of course, but most of it is, and probably more than is generally acknowledged. Some congregants have never heard an affirmation of their work from their church even if they have been regular attendees. Such an affirmation could mean a lot to many of them.

This is especially true as it pertains to the goods and services their work provides to others. People generally understand that their church teaches them to treat other people well and to behave with integrity, but they often have trouble understanding the religious connection or value in the product of their work. By not seeing this connection, the integration they seek between their work and their faith remains elusive, and their faith or spirituality risks being confined to limited areas of their lives.

There can be several different reasons for this. Perhaps their church has discussed work-related issues in sermons but the individual does not attend services often enough to hear them. Or perhaps they attend a church that ignores their work life or have encountered hostility to business or to their particular occupation.

Churches sometimes inadvertently give the impression that the primary opportunity for contributing to others' well-being is through church or charity projects rather than through the daily work of the congregants. This can give the impression that their daily work is not as important as church work. Even in churches where vocational skills are valued, there can be a tendency to point to exemplars who have either left their occupation to use their vocational skills for charity or church work, or have added to their business a social justice activity (such as funding a homeless employment project) that has no direct bearing on their main work. These activities can have considerable value, but if all our examples of people using their skills for good involve individuals who have stepped outside their ordinary jobs to do something else, what does that say to those of us who work hard at more ordinary jobs?

The Bible has resources that can help us affirm the value of daily work. As mentioned, I particularly like the concept of shalom as a way to identify the contribution our work should, and often does, make to the flourishing of society. Shalom can also provide a criterion with which to make trade-offs between different values and goals.

Connect With the Faith or Spirituality of the Participants

I do not believe that a faith and work program is the proper venue for evangelism. Our goal should be to help people see how their own faith or spirituality can inform and support them in their work, help them experience a deeper sense of divine purpose, and see how their work can contribute to the well-being of other people.

Most people have a deep, intuitive religiosity that is usually kept hidden but nevertheless has a potentially profound effect on their approach to life. This deep religiosity (some might call it spirituality) might or might not correspond to the religious beliefs they acknowledge publicly. It is often subconscious but seems to emerge into conscious awareness from time to time. When it does emerge, it can be a powerful source of insight, strength, and resilience in our work lives.

We need to be careful, however; if we are serious about engaging people from outside the church, we must avoid inadvertently sending signals that the program is only designed for people whose beliefs fit a particular theological template. Many people outside the church are quite sensitive about this issue and might think they see signs of this even when that is not the organizers' intention. This is one reason why people are sometimes reluctant to attend church-based programs (this is less of a problem with online offerings where people can be anonymous and easily exit).

This does not mean that we can never discuss religious or spiritual topics with people who come from outside the church. Many of these people pray frequently and occasionally ponder the great mysteries of existence. They might also enjoy talking about spiritual or religious matters, as long as they do not feel the purpose of the discussion is to change their views or to remake them in some way. They often also appreciate learning about and engaging in Christian spiritual practices.

Business school professor Laura Nash and pastor Scotty McLennan offer an intriguing framework for understanding this issue as it pertains to the workplace.[111] They suggest that religion operates on three levels of engagement. The first level, which they call espoused religion, is concerned with people having the correct beliefs and religious allegiances. Espoused religion taken too far is often frowned upon in the workplace and in many social settings outside the church and is usually counterproductive.

Nash and McLennan call the second level catalytic religion. This includes experiential and transformational spiritual practices (e.g., prayer, meditation) that people find helpful in their day-to-day work. It is at this level that so-called secular spirituality programs have been the most effective.

The third level is what they call foundational religion. This involves tapping into the wisdom and foundational stories of religion in ways that help us think about the sacred. It is at this level that Christianity might have the greatest underutilized value for people in the workplace, especially if it can be combined with the catalytic level while avoiding the traps of espoused religion.

In any case, a faith and work program will be far more effective if it can engage the participant's own intuitive faith or spirituality without coming across as a program of evangelism.

Use Language That Connects With the Workplace

Different spheres of life use different terminology. The logical rules and structural relationships between the words can be quite different as well. This can create a problem when we are trying to connect our faith and our work—two domains that use different languages—especially when we are not conscious of the differences. Developing the ability to use language that crosses the domains can be very useful.

Compare the expression of values in business and in the "typical" church. There is overlap; for example, altruistic concerns for others can be found in both, as can a desire for integrity. But there are also differences. A typical church might highlight the relationship of concepts such as sin, forgiveness, and divine grace. A business might reflect more concern with producing value in the form of goods and services, exchanging products with others through the market, and serving customers. When confronted with the problem of hunger, churches might highlight volunteer projects and donations, while business logic might look for ways to produce and distribute more food. Both are necessary but sound quite different even though there is considerable conceptual overlap.

It makes sense to use different terminology in different spheres. The problem comes about when the language of one crowds out the language of the other, especially if we are trying to encourage integration. We need to combine the language of the two spheres and talk of the religious and spiritual significance of creating goods and services, building healthy job-creating businesses, encouraging productive collaborative relationships, and weathering the storms of the marketplace.

The transcendent, all-pervasive, fully immanent God is not confined to one sphere of life. Spirituality should not be limited either and our language needs to reflect this.

Take Advantage of Online Opportunities

Many people have become accustomed to online events and activities, including those of a religious nature; this presents additional opportunities for faith and work ministry. We might think of people carrying part of their church with them on their smartphones.

We should first acknowledge that in-person environments have obvious advantages over online. Most people enjoy being physically present during events and might be more engaged when they are. In-person interactions can be more conducive to forming relationships. And people are less easily distracted when the speaker is standing in front of them in the same room.

But the online environment has advantages as well. Online options are, in some cases, easier for working people with long commutes to attend. Programs can be customized to meet smaller niches but with greater geographical coverage. Relationships and discussions can be maintained despite travel schedules.

One of the important considerations when designing online programs or components of programs is to think through the capabilities and opportunities that are native to the online environment. We need to do more than transfer in-person activities to an online channel; people engage with online media differently than they do in-person offerings. This presents both challenges and opportunities.

Final Thoughts

Churches have an opportunity to help people both inside and outside the church in an important area of their lives. A church that does this in a helpful, constructive manner can engage with and help a much broader segment of the population than it currently reaches.

References

Endnotes

Internet reference links valid as of January 20, 2023.

1. Kenneth I. Pargament, "Spirituality as an Irreducible Human Motivation and Process" in *International Journal for the Psychology of Religion* (2013) pp. 271-272.
2. Ibid., p. 272.
3. Kenneth I. Pargament, *Spiritually Integrated Psychotherapy: Understanding and Addressing the Sacred* (New York: The Guilford Press, 2007) Kindle Loc. 777.
4. The Enuma Elish can be found at https://www.sacred-texts.com/ane/enuma.htm.
5. All scripture passages are from the *New Revised Standard Version Bible*, © 1989 by the Division of Christian Education of the National Council of the Churches of Christ in the U.S.A. Used by permission. All rights reserved.
6. Paul Tillich, *Systematic Theology: Three Volumes in One* (Chicago, Il.: The University of Chicago Press, 1951/1967) Vol. 1, p. 156. See also Paul Tillich, *The Courage to Be (The Terry Lecture Series)* (New Haven, CT: Yale University Press, 1952).
7. Teresa Amabile and Steven Kramer, *The Purpose Principle: Using Small Wins to Ignite Joy, Engagement and Creativity at Work* (Boston, Mass: Harvard Business Review Press, 2011) p.3.
8. Martin E.P. Seligman, *Flourish: A Visionary New Understanding of Happiness and Well-Being* (New York: Free Press, 2011) Kindle Loc. 285-375.
9. Stewart I. Donaldson, Llewellyn Ellardus van Zyl, and Scott I. Donaldson, "PERMA+4: A Framework for Work-Related Wellbeing,

Performance and Positive Organizational Psychology 2.0" in *Frontiers in Psychology* (January 2022) Volume 12, Article 817244, p. 1.

10. Edward L. Deci and Richard M. Ryan (eds). *Handbook of Self Determination Research* (Rochester, NY: University of Rochester Press, 2002) pp. 6-8.

11. Robert J. Vallerand, *The Psychology of Passion: A Dualistic Model* (New York: Oxford University Press, 2015) pp. 62-66.

12. Ibid.

13. Ibid., p. 208.

14. A good discussion of these issues can be found in: Theology of Work Project, *Theology of Work Bible Commentary, Vol. 1: Genesis through Deuteronomy* (Peabody, Mass: Hendrickson, 2015) pp. 110-113, 126-127. See also *Vol. II: Joshua Through Song of Songs*, pp. 35-36.

15. Ibid., p. 136.

16. Richard S. Lazarus, *Stress and Emotion: A New Synthesis* (New York: Springer Publishing Company, 1999) p. 71.

17. Ibid., p. 76.

18. Scott Symington, *Freedom from Anxious Thoughts & Feelings: A Two-Step Mindfulness Approach for Moving Beyond Fear and Worry* (Oakland, CA: New Harbinger Publishing, 2019).

19. Ibid.

20. http://faithandenterprise.org

21. Kenneth I. Pargament, *The Psychology of Religion and Coping: Theory, Research, and Practice*, (New York: The Guilford Press, 1997) p. 312.

22. Ibid., p. 180.

23. Explanations for the meaning of "selah" remain speculative. It might have been an instruction to the musicians or a call for a liturgical action.

24. Christina Maslach and Michael P. Leiter, *The Truth About Burnout: How Organizations Cause Personal Stress and What to Do About It* (San Francisco: Jossey-Bass, 1997) Kindle Edition Loc. 219-230.

25. Ibid., loc 125-215.

26. Ibid., loc. 232.

27. http://faithandenterprise.org. See also Sam Alibrando, *Follow the*

Yellow Brick Road: How To Change For the Better When Life Gives You Its Worst (Lincoln, NE: iUniverse, 2007), and Sam Alibrando, *The 3 Dimensions of Emotions: Finding the Balance of Power, Heart, and Mindfulness in All of Your Relationships* (Wayne, NJ: Career Press, 2016).

28. Matthew J. Rossano, "The Moral Faculty: Does Religion Promote 'Moral Expertise'?" in *The International Journal for the Psychology of Religion* (Taylor & Francis Group, 2008 #18) pp. 177-178.

29. Christopher Peterson and Martin E.P. Seligman, *Character Strengths and Virtues: A Handbook and Classification* (Oxford, UK: Oxford University Press, 2004).

30. Sarah McKibben, "Grit and the Greater Good: A Conversation Angela Duckworth" in *Educational Leadership*, October 2018, pp. 40-41. See also *Angela Duckworth on Character Development* (Video produced by John Templeton Foundation, 2019) https://www.youtube.com/watch?v=_uGjT5RRdxU.

31. Elizabeth E. Umphress and John B. Bingham, "When Employees Do Bad Things for Good Reasons: Examining Unethical Pro-Organizational Behaviors," *Organization Science* (Vol. 22, No. 3, May-June 2011) pp. 622.

32. Fred Luthans, Carolyn M. Youssef, and Bruce J. Avolio, *Psychological Capital: Developing the Human Competitive Edge* (Oxford, UK: Oxford University Press, 2007) Kindle Edition, p. 196.

33. Peterson aand Seligman, p.199.

34. Ibid., p. 29.

35. Christopher R. Rate, "Defining the Features of Courage: A Search for Meaning" in C.L.S. Pury and S.J. Lopez (eds.) *The Psychology of Courage: Modern Research on an Ancient Virtue*, American Psychological Association (2010) Chapter 3, p. 63.

36. Monica C. Worline, "Understanding the Role of Courage in Social Life" in C.L.S. Pury and S.J. Lopez (eds.) *The Psychology of Courage: Modern Research on an Ancient Virtue*, American Psychological Association (2010) Chapter 11, p. 210.

37. Ibid., pp. 217-222.

38. Psychologist Stanley Rachman gathered and conducted studies

of people in very high-risk occupations and found that confidence in one's training and expertise made a very important contribution to one's courage. S.J. Rachman, "Courage: A Psychological Perspective" in C.L.S. Pury and S.J. Lopez (eds.) *The Psychology of Courage: Modern Research on an Ancient Virtue*, American Psychological Association (2010) Chapter 5, pp. 91-107.

39. See for example Monica C. Worline and Jane E. Dutton, *Awakening Compassion at Work: The Quiet Power That Elevates People and Organizations*, Berret-Koehler Publishers (Oakland, CA: 2017) p. 4-5.

40. Ibid., p. 33.

41. Ibid., p. 15.

42. Sometimes our good intentions do not have the effect for which we hope. Barbara Oakley and colleagues have written extensively about the times when ostensibly good intentions cause harm. In extreme cases, this can be called pathological altruism: "Pathological altruism might be thought of as any behavior or tendency in which either the stated aim or the implied motivation is to promote the welfare of others. But, instead of overall beneficial outcomes, the 'altruism' instead has irrational and substantial negative consequences to the other, even to the self." Barbara Oakley, Ariel Knafo, Guruprasad Madhaven, and Michel McGrath (eds), *Pathological Altruism* (Oxford, UK: Oxford University Press, 2012) p. 4.

43. See, for example, Jim Collins, *Good to Great: Why Some Companies Make the Leap and Others Don't* (New York: Harper Collins, 2001).

44. Robert Emmons, *The Psychology of Ultimate Concerns: Motivation and Spirituality in Personality* (New York: The Guilford Press, 1999) p. 171.

45. June Tangney, "Humility: Theoretical Perspectives, Empirical Findings and Directions for Future Research" in: *Journal of Clinical and Social Psychology* (2000, #19) pp. 73-74.

46. Peter C. Hill, http://faithandenterprise.org (public lecture), 2018.

47. Peterson and Seligman, p. 478.

48. Fred Luthans, "The Need For and Meaning of Positive Organizational Behavior," in *Journal of Organizational Behavior*, Vol. 23, No. 6 (September 2002) p. 702. As quoted in Fred Luthans,

Organizational Behavior: An Evidence-Based Approach, 12th Edition (New York: McGraw-Hill Irvin, 2011) p. 218.

49. C.R. Snyder, *The Psychology of Hope: You Can Get There From Here* (New York: The Free Press, 1994) pp. 15-23.

50. Jennifer S. Cheavens and David B. Feldman, *The Science and Application of Positive Psychology* (New York: Cambridge University Press, 2022), p. 375. See also Jennifer S. Cheavens, *Hope Therapy and a Novel Approach to Psychopathology Interventions* (online lecture/ interview), International Positive Psychology Association, October 17, 2019. For a video summary: https://vimeo.com/405920679.

51. From the Lord's Prayer section of *Martin Luther's Small Catechism*, as presented by the Evangelical Lutheran Synod at https://els.org/ beliefs/luthers-small-catechism/part-3-the-lords-prayer/.

52. Denise Daniels and Shannon Vandewarker, *Working in the Presence of God: Spiritual Practices for Everyday Work* (Peabody, MA: Hendrickson Publishers, 2019) Kindle version, Loc. 673.

53. G.E.H. Palmer, Philip Sherrard, and Kallistos Ware (eds. and trans.), *The Philokalia: The Complete Text Compiled by St. Nikodimos of the Holy Mountain and S. Makarios of Corinth, Volume I* (London: Faber and Faber, 1979) p. 15.

54. John Cassian, Translation and Notes by Edgar C.S. Gibson, *The Conferences of John Cassian, from A Select Library of Nicene and Post-Nicene Fathers of the Christian Church* (New York, 1894/2010) Kindle Edition, p. 204. John Cassian was an early monk and theologian who helped to bring Christianity to Europe.

55. I have not been able to find the reference, but see John Wortley, "Prayer and the Desert Fathers", in *The Coming of the Comforter: When, Where, and to Whom?* https://www.researchgate.net/ publication/337834707_Prayer_and_the_Desert_Fathers, p.115.

56. For more practices, see Robert A. Emmons, T*he Little Book of Gratitude: Create a Life of Happiness and Well-Being by Giving Thanks* (New York: Hachette, 2014); for background, see Robert A. Emmons and Michael E. McCullogh (eds.) *The Psychology of Gratitude (Series in Affective Science)* (New York: Oxford University Press, 2004).

57. Guigo II (auth.), Edmund College (ed. and trans.), and James Walsh (ed. and trans.) *Guigo II: The Ladder for Monks and Twelve Meditations*

(Collegeville, MN: Cistercian Publications,1979) pp. 67-68.

58. Daniels and Vandewarker, loc. 1133.

59. Gabriela Tonietto and Selin Malkoc, "The Calendar Mindset: Scheduling Takes the Fun Out and Puts the Work In" in *Journal of Marketing Research* Vol. LIII (December 2016), pp. 922–936.

60. Robert N. Bellah, Richard Madsen, William M. Sullivan, Ann Swidler, Steven M. Tipton, *Habits of The Heart: Individualism and Commitment in American Life (Updated Version)* (Berkeley, CA: University of California Press, New York: Harper Collins, 1996/1985) Kindle Edition, Loc. 1497-1506.

61. Amy Wrzesniewski, Paul Rozin, and Gwen Bennett, "Working, Playing, and Eating: Making the Most of Most Moments" in C L.M. Hayes and J. Haidt (eds.) *Flourishing: Positive Psychology and the Life Well-Lived*, (Washington, DC: American Psychological Association, 2003) p. 189.

62. Amy Wrzesniewski, "Callings" in Kim Cameron and Gretchen Spreitzer (eds) *The Oxford Handbook of Positive Organizational Scholarship* (New York: Oxford University Press, 2011) p. 47.

63. Douglas T. Hall and Dawn E. Chandler, "Psychological Success: When the Career is Calling" in *Journal of Organizational Behavior* (2005), p. 160.

64. Ibid.

65. Hall and Chandler, p.163.

66. Shoshana R. Dobrow and Jennifer Tosti-Kharas, "Calling: The Development of a Scale Measure" in *Personnel Psychology* Winter 2011, Vol. 64 Issue 4, p. 1001.

67. Bryan J. Dik and Ryan D. Duffy, *Make Your Job a Calling: How the Psychology of Vocation Can Change Your Life at Work* (West Conshohoken, PA: Templeton Press, 2012).

68. Ibid., pp. 7-8.

69. Ibid.

70. Ibid., p.11.

71. Ibid., p. 9.

72. Ibid., p. 50.

73. Ibid., p. 13.

74. James Hillman, *The Soul's Code: In Search of Character and Calling*

(New York: Ballantine Books, 1996) p. 6.

75. For summaries of research on the benefits of calling, see: Bryan J. Dik and Ryan D. Duffy, "Strategies for Discerning and Living a Calling" in P.J. Hurting, M.L. Savickas, and W.B. Walsh (eds.), *APA Handbook of Career Intervention: Vol. 2. Applications* (American Psychological Association, 2015) Chapter 23; and Wrzesniewski, "Callings," p.51.

76. Dik and Duffy (2015), p. 308.

77. Justin M. Berg, Amy Wrzesniewski, and Jane E. Dutton, "Job Crafting and Meaningful Work" in Bryan J. Dik, Z. S. Byrne, and Michael F. Steger (eds.) *Purpose and Meaning in the Workplace* (American Psychological Association, 2013) pp. 81- 82.

78. Justin M. Berg, Adam M. Grant, and Victoria Johnson, "When Callings Are Calling: Crafting Work and Leisure in Pursuit of Unanswered Callings" in *Organization Science*, (Vol. 21, No. 5) September-October 2010, pp. 982-984.

79. Teresa M. Cardador and Brianna B. Caza, "Relational and Identity Perspectives on Healthy Versus Unhealthy Pursuit of Callings," *Journal of Career Assessment*, 2012, pp. 338-353 (quote from p. 349).

80. Shoshana R. Dobrow, "Extreme Subjective Career Success: A New Integrated View of Having a Calling," (Academy of Management Best Conference Paper, 2004) p. B5.

81. Tod Bolsinger, Fuller Seminary professor and Vice President of Vocation and Formation believes that developing a calling is part of the formation process, and that "our vocation is not truly found until we are fit for it." Tod Bolsinger, "Formed, Not Found," Fuller Theological Seminary-Fuller Studio (https://fullerstudio.fuller.edu/formed-not-found/).

82. Bryan J. Dik, Ryan D. Duffy, and Brandy M. Eldridge, "Calling and Vocation in Career Counseling: Recommendations for Promoting Meaningful Work," *Professional Psychology: Research and Practice* (Vol. 40, No. 6) pp. 628. See also: Bryan J. Dik and Ryan D. Duffy, "Strategies for Discerning and Living a Calling" in P.J. Hurting, M.L. Savickas, and W.B. Walsh (eds.), *APA Handbook of Career Intervention: Vol. 2. Applications* (American Psychological Association,

2015) Chapter 23.

83. Bryan J. Dik and Ryan D. Duffy, "Calling and Vocation at Work: Definitions and Prospects for Research and Practice," *The Counseling Psychologist* (April 2009, Vol. 37, No. 3) p. 441.

84. Abraham Zaleznik, "Managers and Leaders: Are They Different?" *Harvard Business Review* (January 2004 - reprinted from 1977).

85. Ibid.

86. Ibid.

87. Ibid.

88. *APA Dictionary of Psychology* (Washington, DC: American Psychological Association, 2020) https://dictionary.apa.org/narcissism.

89. Manfred F.R. Kets de Vries and Elisabet Engellau, "A Clinical Approach to the Dynamics of Leadership and Executive Transformation" in Nitin Nohria and Rakesh Khurana (eds.) *Handbook of Leadership Theory and Practice: A Harvard Business School Centennial Colloquium* (Boston, MA: Harvard Business Press, 2010) pp. 194-195.

90. Ibid., p. 193.

91. Ibid., p. 194.

92. Cf. Manfred F.R. Kets de Vries, *The Leader on the Couch: A Clinical Approach to Changing People and Organizations* (San Francisco, CA: Jossey-Bass, 2006) Chapter 2.

93. Kets de Vries and Engellau, p.195.

94. Bruce J. Avolio, "Pursuing Authentic Leadership Development" in Nitin Nohria and Rakesh Khurana (eds.) *Handbook of Leadership Theory and Practice: A Harvard Business School Centennial Colloquium* (Boston, MA: Harvard Business Press, 2010) pp. 742-745.

95. Melissa Trivisonno and Julian Barling, "A Passion for Leadership" in Robert J. Vallerand and Nathalie Houlfort (eds), *Passion for Work: Theory, Research, and Applications* (New York: Oxford University Press, 2019) p. 413.

96. Business scholars Jennifer Chapman and Jessica Kennedy refer to this as the "paradox of leadership" and discuss some of the implications. Jennifer A. Chapman and Jessica A. Kennedy, "Psychological Perspectives on Leadership" in Nitin Nohria and Rakesh Khurana (eds.) *Handbook of*

Leadership Theory and Practice: A Harvard Business School Centennial Colloquium (Boston, Mass: Harvard Business Press, 2010) pp. 163-164.

98. See also: Theology of Work Project (Vol.1) p. 21.

99. Ibid., pp. 103-104.

100. Ibid., pp. 126-127.

101. Theology of Work Project, *Theology of Work Bible Commentary*, Vol. 4: Matthew Through Acts (Peabody, Mass: Hendrickson, 2014) pp. 28, 60, 75.

102. Thomas L. Friedman, *Thank You for Being Late: An Optimist's Guide to Thriving in an Age of Accelerations* (New York: Farar, Straus and Giroux, 2016) pp. 227-231.

103. Ibid., p. 229.

104. Mihaly Csikszentmihalyi, *Flow: The Psychology of Optimal Experience* (New York: Harper Collins, 2008/1990) p. 71.

105. Ibid., pp. 49-67.

106. Ibid.

107. https://www.madetoflourish.org

108. https://www.faithandworkla.com/courses

109. https://www.partnersworldwide.org

110. https://depree.org/life-for-leaders/

111. Laura Nash and Scotty McLennan, *Church on Sunday, Work on Monday: The Challenge of Fusing Christian Values with Business Life* (San Francisco: Jossey-Bass, 2001) pp. 224-237.

Bibliography

Alibrando, Sam. *Follow the Yellow Brick Road: How To Change For the Better When Life Gives You Its Worst.* Lincoln, NE: iUniverse, 2007.

Alibrando, Sam. *The 3 Dimensions of Emotions: Finding the Balance of Power, Heart, and Mindfulness in All of Your Relationships.* Wayne, NJ: Career Press, 2016.

Amabile, Teresa and Steven Kramer. *The Purpose Principle: Using Small Wins to Ignite Joy, Engagement and Creativity at Work.* Boston, Mass: Harvard Business Review Press, 2011.

APA Dictionary of Psychology. Washington, DC: American Psychological Association, 2020, https://dictionary.apa.org/.

Ashforth, Blake E. and Glen E. Kreiner. "Profane or Profound? Finding Meaning in Dirty Work." In *Purpose and Meaning in the Workplace.* Edited by Bryan Dik, Zinta S. Byrne, and Michael Steger. Washington, DC: American Psychological Association, 2013.

Avolio, Bruce J. "Pursuing Authentic Leadership Development." In *Handbook of Leadership Theory and Practice: A Harvard Business School Centennial Colloquium.* Edited by Nitin Nohria and Rakesh Khurana. Boston, MA: Harvard Business Press, 2010.

Banks, Robert. *Redeeming the Routines: Bringing Theology to Life.* Grand Rapids, MI: Baker Academic, 2001.

Barna Group. *Christians at Work.* Ventura, CA: Barna Group, 2018.

Bellah, Robert N., Richard Madsen, William M. Sullivan, Ann Swidler, Steven M. Tipton. *Habits of The Heart: Individualism and Commitment in American Life (Updated Version)* New York: Harper Collins, 1996/1985.

Berg, Justin M., Adam M. Grant, and Victoria Johnson. "When Callings Are Calling: Crafting Work and Leisure in Pursuit of Unanswered Callings" in *Organization Science* Vol. 21, No. 5 (September-October 2010); pp. 973-994.

Berg, Justin M., Amy Wrzesniewski, and Jane E. Dutton. "Job Crafting and Meaningful Work." In *Purpose and Meaning in the Workplace.* Edited by Bryan J. Dik, Z.S. Byrne, and Michael F. Steger. Washington, DC: American Psychological Association, 2013.

Bolsinger, Tod. "Formed, Not Found." Fuller Theological Seminary-Fuller Studio. https://fullerstudio.fuller.edu/formed-not-found/.

Bolsinger, Tod. *Canoeing the Mountains: Christian Leadership in Uncharted Territory.* Expanded edition. Downers Grove, IL: IVP Books, 2018.

Buszka, Sharlene G. and Timothy Ewest. *Integrating Christian Faith and Work: Individual, Occupational, and Organizational Influences and Strategies.* Cham, Switzerland: Palgrave Macmillan, 2020.

Cardador, Teresa M., and Brianna B. Caza. "Relational and Identity Perspectives on Healthy Versus Unhealthy Pursuit of Callings," *Journal of Career Assessment* 20:3 (2012): pp. 338–353.

Cassian, John. In *The Conferences of John Cassian*, from *A Select Library of Nicene and Post-Nicene Fathers of the Christian Church*. Translation and Notes by Edgar C.S. Gibson. New York, 1894/2010.

Chapman, Jennifer A. and Jessica A. Kennedy. "Psychological Perspectives on Leadership." In *Handbook of Leadership Theory and Practice: A Harvard Business School Centennial Colloquium*. Edited by Nitin Nohria and Rakesh Khurana. Boston, MA: Harvard Business Press, 2010.

Cheavens, Jennifer S. *Hope Therapy and a Novel Approach to Psychopathology Interventions* (online lecture/interview). International Positive Psychology Association, October 17, 2019.

Cheavens, Jennifer S. and David B. Feldman. *The Science and Application of Positive Psychology*. New York : Cambridge University Press, 2022.

Claar, Victor V. and Robin J. Klay. *Economics in Christian Perspective: Theory, Policy and Life Choices*. Downers Grove, IL: IVP Academic, 2007.

College, Edmund (ed. and trans.) and James Walsh (ed. and trans.) *Guigo II: The Ladder for Monks and Twelve Meditations*. Collegeville, MN: Cistercian Publications, 1979.

Collins, Jim. *Good to Great: Why Some Companies Make the Leap and Others Don't*. New York: Harper Collins, 2001.

Crawford, Matthew B. "The Case for Working With Your Hands." *The New York Times Magazine,* May 21, 2009.

Csikszentmihalyi, Mihaly. *Flow: The Psychology of Optimal Experience*. New York: Harper Collins, 2008/1990.

Daniels, Denise and Shannon Vandewarker. *Working in the Presence of God: Spiritual Practices for Everyday Work.* Peabody, MA: Hendrickson Publishers, 2019.

Deci, Edward L. and Richard M. Ryan. (eds). *Handbook of Self Determination Research.* Rochester, N.Y.: University of Rochester Press, 2002.

Dik, Bryan J. and Ryan D. Duffy. "Calling and Vocation at Work: Definitions and Prospects for Research and Practice." In *The Counseling Psychologist* Vol. 37, No. 3 (April 2009); p. 441.

Dik, Bryan J., Ryan D. Duffy, and Brandy M. Eldridge. "Calling and Vocation in Career Counseling: Recommendations for Promoting Meaningful Work." In *Professional Psychology Research and Practice* Vol. 40, No. 6 (December 2009): pp. 625-632.

Dik, Bryan J. and Ryan D. Duffy. *Make Your Job a Calling: How the Psychology of Vocation Can Change Your Life at Work.* West Conshohoken, PA: Templeton Press, 2012.

Dik, Bryan J. (ed.), Zinta S. Byrne (ed.), and Michael Steger (ed.). *Purpose and Meaning in the Workplace.* Washington, DC: American Psychological Association, 2013.

Dik, Bryan J. and Ryan D. Duffy. "Strategies for Discerning and Living a Calling." In *APA Handbook of Career Intervention: Vol. 2. Applications.* Edited by P.J. Hurting, M.L. Savickas, and W.B. Walsh. Washington, DC: American Psychological Association, 2015.

Dobrow, Shoshana R. "Extreme Subjective Career Success: A New Integrated View of Having a Calling." Academy of Management Best Conference Paper, 2004.

Dobrow, Shoshana R. and Jennifer Tosti-Kharas. "Calling: The Development of a Scale Measure." In *Personnel Psychology* (Winter 2011) Vol. 64, Issue 4.

Donaldson, Scott I., Joo Young Lee, Stewart I. Donaldson. "Evaluating Positive Psychology Interventions at Work." *International Journal of Applied Positive Psychology.* (September 10, 2019). https://doi.org/10.1007/s41042-019-00021-8.

Donaldson, Stewart I., Llewellyn Ellardus van Zyl, and Scott I. Donaldson. "PERMA+4: A Framework for Work-Related Wellbeing, Performance and Positive Organizational Psychology 2.0." In *Frontiers in Psychology* (January 2022) Volume 12, Article 817244.

Duckworth, Angela. *Angela Duckworth on Character Development* Video produced by John Templeton Foundation (2019) https://www.youtube.com/watch?v=_uGjT5RRdxU.

Duckworth, Angela. "How and Why to Develop Character." *Positive Psychology Leader Series* (online lecture/interview), International Positive Psychology Association (December 19, 2019.)

Economic Wisdom Project. *A Christian Vision for Flourishing Communities.* Oikonomia Network, 2015.

Emmons, Robert A. and Michael E. McCullogh (eds.). *The Psychology of Gratitude (Series in Affective Science).* New York: Oxford University Press, 2004.

Emmons, Robert A. T*he Little Book of Gratitude: Create a Life of Happiness and Well-Being by Giving Thanks.* New York: Hachette, 2014.

Emmons, Robert. *The Psychology of Ultimate Concerns: Motivation and Spirituality in Personality*. New York: The Guilford Press, 1999.

Ewest, Timothy (ed.). *Faith and Work: Christian Perspectives, Research, and Insights Into the Movement*. Charlotte, North Carolina: Information Age Publishing, 2018.

Friedman, Thomas L. *Thank You for Being Late: An Optimist's Guide to Thriving in an Age of Accelerations*. New York: Farar, Straus and Giroux, 2016.

Gallup, Inc. *The State of the American Workplace*. Washington, DC: Gallup, 2017.

Gonzalez, Justo. *Faith and Wealth: A History of Early Christian Ideas on the Origin, Significance, and Use of Money*. Eugene, Oregon: Wipf and Stock, 2002.

Graham, W. Fred. *The Constructive Revolutionary: John Calvin and His Socio-Economic Impact*. Richmond, VA: John Knox Press, 1971.

Hall, Douglas T. and Dawn E. Chandler. "Psychological Success: When the Career is Calling." In *Journal of Organizational Behavior* Vol. 26, No. 2 (March 2005).

Heyne, Paul. "Economics Scientists and Skeptical Theologians." *Online Library of Liberty*. Indianapolis: Liberty Fund, 2008.

Hill, Peter C. *Work Life Forum* (Public Lecture at La Cañada Presbyterian Church). La Cañada, California, September 2018.

Hill, Peter C. (ed.) and Bryan J. Dik (ed.). *Psychology of Religion and Workplace Spirituality*. Charlotte, North Carolina: Information Age Publishing, 2012.

Hillman, James. *The Soul's Code: In Search of Character and Calling.* New York: Ballantine Books, 1996.

Hurting, M.L. Savickas, and W.B. Walsh (eds.), *APA Handbook of Career Intervention: Vol. 2. Applications* (American Psychological Association, 2015) Chapter 23.

Keller, Timothy with Katherine Leary Alsdorf. *Every Good Endeavor: Connecting Your Work to God's Work.* New York: Penguin Books, 2012.

Kets de Vries, Manfred F.R. *The Leader on the Couch: A Clinical Approach to Changing People and Organizations.* San Francisco, CA: Jossey-Boss, 2006.

Kets de Vries, Manfred F.R. and Elisabet Engellau. "A Clinical Approach to the Dynamics of Leadership and Executive Transformation." In *Handbook of Leadership Theory and Practice: A Harvard Business School Centennial Colloquium.* Edited by Nitin Nohria and Rakesh Khurana. Boston, MA: Harvard Business Press, 2010.

Kliewer, Wendy. "Resiliency." In *Baker Encyclopedia of Pastoral Counseling.* Peter C. Hill (ed.) and David G. Benner (ed.). Grand Rapids, MI: Baker Books, 1999.

Kuyper, Abraham, and James D. Bratt (ed). *Abraham Kuyper: A Centennial Reader.* Grand Rapids, MI: Eerdmans, 1998.

Kuyper, Abraham. *Lectures on Calvinism.* Grand Rapids, MI: Eerdmans, 1943.

Kuyper, Abraham. *The Problem of Poverty.* Sioux Center, IA: Dordt College Theological Press, 1992.

Lazarus, Richard S. *Stress and Emotion: A New Synthesis*. New York: Springer Publishing Company, 1999.

Luthans, Fred. "The Need For and Meaning of Positive Organizational Behavior. In *Journal of Organizational Behavior*. Vol. 23, No. 6 (September 2002).

Luthans, Fred. *Organizational Behavior: An Evidence-Based Approach*, 12th Edition. New York: McGraw-Hill Irvin, 2011.

Luthans, Fred, Carolyn M. Youssef, and Bruce J. Avolio. *Psychological Capital: Developing the Human Competitive Edge*. Oxford, UK: Oxford University Press, 2007.

Luther, Martin. *Martin Luther's Small Catechism*. Lutheran Evangelical Synod. https://els.org/beliefs/luthers-small-catechism/part-3-the-lords-prayer/.

Maslach, Christina, and Michael P. Leiter. *The Truth About Burnout: How Organizations Cause Personal Stress and What to Do About It*. San Francisco: Jossey-Bass, 1997.

McKee, Elsie. "The Character and Significance of John Calvin's Teaching on Social and Economics Issues." In *John Calvin Rediscovered: The Impact of His Social and Economic Thought*. Edited by Edward Dommen and James D. Bratt. Louisville, KY: Westminister John Knox Press, 2007.

McKibben, Sarah. "Grit and the Greater Good: A Conversation Angela Duckworth." In *Educational Leadership*. October 2018.

Messenger, William. "Calling & Vocation: Overview." *Theology of Work Project*. https://www.theologyofwork.org/key-topics/vocation-overview-article.

Miller, David W. *God at Work: The History and Promise of the Faith at Work Movement.* New York: Oxford, 2006.

Nash, Laura and Scotty McLennan. *Church on Sunday, Work on Monday: The Challenge of Fusing Christian Values with Business Life.* San Francisco: Jossey-Bass, 2001.

Nelson, Tom. *Work Matters: Connecting Sunday Worship to Monday Work.* Wheaton, IL: Crossway, 2011.

Nelson, Tom. *The Economics of Neighborly Love: Investing in Your Community's Compassion and Capacity.* Downers Grove: IVP Books, 2017.

New Revised Standard Version Bible. Division of Christian Education of the National Council of the Churches of Christ in the U.S.A., 1989.

Novak, Michael. *Business as a Calling: Work and the Examined Life.* New York: The Free Press, 1996.

Oakley, Barbara, Ariel Knafo, Guruprasad Madhaven, and Michel McGrath, (eds), *Pathological Altruism.* Oxford, UK: Oxford University Press, 2012.

Palmer, G.E.H., Philip Sherrard, and Kallistos Ware, (eds. and trans.), *The Philokalia: The Complete Text Compiled by St. Nikodimos of the Holy Mountain and S. Makarios of Corinth, Volume I.* London: Faber and Faber, 1979.

Pargament, Kenneth I. *The Psychology of Religion and Coping: Theory, Research, and Practice*, The Guilford Press (New York: 1997).

Pargament, Kenneth I. *Spiritually Integrated Psychotherapy: Understanding and Addressing the Sacred.* New York: The Guilford Press, 2007.

Pargament, Kenneth I. "Spirituality as an Irreducible Human Motivation and Process" in *International Journal for the Psychology of Religion 23*(4),(2013).

Peterson, Christopher and Martin E.P. Seligman. *Character Strengths and Virtues: A Handbook and Classification.* Oxford, UK: Oxford University Press, 2004.

Pew Research Center. *The State of American Jobs: How the shifting economic landscape is reshaping work and society and affecting the way people think about the skills and training they need to get ahead.* Washington, DC: Pew Research Center, 2016.

Plantinga, Cornelius Jr.. *Not the Way It's Supposed to Be: A Breviary of Sin.* Grand Rapids, MI: Eerdmans, 1995.

Rate, Christopher R. "Defining the Features of Courage: A Search for Meaning." In C.L.S. Pury and S. J. Lopez (eds.) *The Psychology of Courage: Modern Research on an Ancient Virtue*, American Psychological Association, 2010.

Rachman, S. J."Courage: A Psychological Perspective." In C.L.S. Pury and S. J. Lopez (eds.) *The Psychology of Courage: Modern Research on an Ancient Virtue*, American Psychological Association, 2010.

Rose, Mike. *The Mind at Work: Valuing the Intelligence of the American Worker.* Tenth Anniversary edition with new preface. New York: Penguin Books, 2014.

Rossano, Matthew J. "The Moral Faculty: Does Religion Promote 'Moral Expertise'?" in *The International Journal for the Psychology of Religion.* 18:3 (2008): pp. 169-194.

Sayers, Dorothy. "Why Work?" *In Letters to a Diminished Church: Passionate Arguments for the Relevance of Christian Doctrine.* Nashville: Thomas Nelson, 2004.

Schwartz, Barry. *Why We Work.* New York: Simon & Schuster (TED Books), 2015.

Seligman, Martin E.P. *Flourish: A Visionary New Understanding of Happiness and Well-Being.* New York: Free Press, 2011.

Sherman, Amy. *Kingdom Calling: Vocational Stewardship for the Common Good.* Downers Grove, IL: IVP Books, 2011.

Smith, Tom W., Michael Davern, Jeremy Freese, Stephen L. Morgan. *General Social Surveys, 1972-2018.* Principal Investigator, Tom W. Smith; Co-Principal Investigators, Michael Davern, Jeremy Freese, and Stephen L. Morgan; Sponsored by National Science Foundation. Chicago: NORC, 2019.

Snyder, C.R. *The Psychology of Hope: You Can Get There From Here.* New York: The Free Press, 1994.

Stander, Hennie. "Economics in the Church Fathers." In *The Oxford Handbook of Christianity and Economics.* Edited by Paul Oslington. New York: Oxford University Press, 2014.

Stark, Rodney. *The Victory of Reason: How Christianity Led to Freedom, Capitalism, and Western Success.* New York: Random House, 2005.

Stevens, R. Paul. *The Other Six Days: Vocation, Work, and Ministry in Biblical Perspective.* Grand Rapids, MI: Eerdmans, 2000.

Symington, Scott. *Freedom from Anxious Thoughts & Feelings: A Two-Step Mindfulness Approach for Moving Beyond Fear and Worry.* Oakland, CA: New Harbinger Publishing, 2019.

Tangney, June Price. "Humility: Theoretical Perspectives, Empirical Findings, and Directions for Future Research" in *Journal of Social and Clinical Psychology*, Vol. 19, No. 1, 2000, pp. 70-82.

Theology of Work Project. *Theology of Work Bible Commentary, Vol. 1: Genesis through Deuteronomy*. Peabody, Mass: Hendrickson, 2015.

Theology of Work Project. *Theology of Work Bible Commentary, Vol. 2: Joshua through Song of Songs*. Peabody, Mass: Hendrickson, 2015.

Theology of Work Project. *Theology of Work Bible Commentary, Vol. 3: Isaiah through Malachi*. Peabody, Mass: Hendrickson, 2016.

Theology of Work Project. *Theology of Work Bible Commentary, Vol. 4; Matthew through Acts*. Peabody, Mass: Hendrickson, 2014.

Theology of Work Project. *Theology of Work Bible Commentary, Vol. 5: Romans through Revelation*. Peabody, Mass: Hendrickson, 2015.

Tillich, Paul. *The Courage to Be (The Terry Lecture Series)*. New Haven, CT: Yale University Press, 1952.

Tillich, Paul. *Systematic Theology: Three Volumes in One*. Chicago, Il.: The University of Chicago Press, 1951/1967.

Tonietto, Gabriela and Selin Malkoc. "The Calendar Mindset: Scheduling Takes the Fun Out and Puts the Work In." In *Journal of Marketing Research* Vol. LIII (December 2016), pp. 922–936.

Trivisonno, Melissa and Julian Barling. "A Passion for Leadership." In *Passion for Work: Theory, Research, and Applications*. Edited by Robert J. Vallerand and Nathalie Houlfort. New York: Oxford University Press, 2019.

Umphress, Elizabeth E. and John Bingham. "When Employees Do Bad Things for Good Reasons: Examining Unethical Pro-Organizational Behaviors," *Organization Science*. Vol. 22, No. 3 (May-June 2011): pp. 621-640.

Vallerand, Robert J. *The Psychology of Passion: A Dualistic Model.* New York: Oxford University Press, 2015.

Van Duzer, Jeff. *Why Business Matters to God: (And What Still Needs to Be Fixed).* Downers Grove, IL: IVP Academic, 2010.

Veith, Gene. *Working for Our Neighbor; A Lutheran Primer on Vocation, Economics and Ordinary Life.* Grand Rapids, MI: Christian's Library Press, 2016.

Volf, Miroslav. *Work in the Spirit: Toward a Theology of Work.* Eugene, OR: Wipf & Stock, 2001.

Worline, Monica C. and Jane E. Dutton. *Awakening Compassion at Work: The Quiet Power That Elevates People and Organizations*, Oakland, CA: Berret-Koehler Publishers, 2017.

Worline, Monica C. "Understanding the Role of Courage in Social Life." In *The Psychology of Courage: Modern Research on an Ancient Virtue.* Edited by C.L.S. Pury and S.J. Lopez. Washington, DC: American Psychological Association, 2010.

Wright, David. *How God Makes the World a Better Place: A Wesleyan Primer on Faith, Work, and Economic Transformation.* Grand Rapids, MI: Christian's Library Press, 2012.

Wrzesniewski, Amy, Paul Rozin, and Gwen Bennett. "Working, Playing, and Eating: Making the Most of Most Moments." In *Flourishing: Positive Psychology and the Life Well-Lived.* Edited by C.L.M. Hayes and J. Haidt. Washington, DC: American Psychological Association, 2003.

Wrzesniewski, Amy. "Callings." *The Oxford Handbook of Positive Organizational Scholarship*. Edited by Kim Cameron and Gretchen Spreitzer. New York: Oxford University Press, 2011.

Zaleznik, Abraham. "Managers and Leaders: Are They Different?" *Harvard Business Review.* January 2004 - reprinted from 1979.

Indexes

The Sacred Meaning of Everyday Work

Scripture Index

Name and Subject Index

About the Author

Rob Tribken has been in business for more than four decades and is the founder of several businesses, including Bestfresh Foods, Inc., a West Coast supplier of packaged food to retail chains. His education includes an MBA from the Harvard Business School and an MA–Theology from Fuller Theological Seminary. He is currently completing a Doctor of Ministry degree in Fuller's Faith, Work, Economics, and Vocation program.

Tribken became interested in the connection between faith and spirituality and work, particularly work in the private sector. Several decades spent working in business combined with several years studying theology and becoming acquainted with organized Christianity convinced him that there is a great need for churches to find better ways to minister to people in the vocational aspects of their lives. In particular, Tribken believes there is a need to affirm the value of commercial vocations and to help people see how their faith and spirituality can help them in their work. This belief led to the founding of the Center for Faith and Enterprise.

Tribken is the author of two sets of curricula designed for small groups: *Transforming Work: Spiritual Renewal In Our Work Lives* and *Questioning Faith: A Conversation for the Open Minded.* He has led retreats, taught classes, and spoken on the subjects of spiritual practices, connecting faith and work, business as a calling, and the role of business in ending poverty. He is also an active member of La Cañada Presbyterian Church in La Cañada, California.

About the Center for Faith and Enterprise

The Center for Faith and Enterprise was launched by Rob Tribken and a group of like-minded California entrepreneurs and business people who wanted to find better ways to help people in business and related fields connect their faith and their work. In October 2018, Tribken sold his business (Bestfresh Foods, Inc.) and became the full-time executive director of the CFE.

Philosophy

As our work has progressed, we have become convinced that many people have a deep, intuitive faith or spirituality that, while often unconscious or latent, can be powerful and life-giving. Our mission is to find ways to help people (including ourselves) tap into this deep resource and allow it to become a source of strength and purpose in our work lives.

Even aside from the income earned, work has important effects on human flourishing, for both good and ill. It can be a source of stress, burnout, boredom, and interpersonal conflict. But work can also provide an opportunity to build friendships, pursue personal growth, contribute to the well-being of others, and develop a sense of purpose. We intend to help people with both the positive and negative aspects of their work.

We also believe that churches and other faith-based entities can play a more important role in helping people deal with their serious work-related issues.

Why "Enterprise"?

Work and enterprise are closely related. We use the word enterprise in our name because it places the emphasis on the positive, forward-looking, constructive aspects of work (and business) and seems to connote a creative spirit of entrepreneurship.

Programs

Work Life Forum: The WLF is a speaker and discussion series designed to help people deal with their serious work-related issues and to do so in a way that is consistent with their own faith or spirituality. Each event includes a speaker who is an expert in the topic as well as time for informal discussion.

Transforming Work Small Group Curriculum: This is a small group curriculum series designed to help people seek spiritual renewal in their work lives and in their workplace. The first two series, published together in one study guide, included twelve sessions. Each session deals with a serious work issue such as stress, integrity, burnout, failure, and opportunity.

The Faith and Enterprise Podcast: The CFE produced thirty-one episodes of this podcast on various topics. We are now in the process of transitioning from a weekly podcast series to a collection of audio recordings organized by topic. These will be updated periodically.

Retreats: The CFE has conducted three retreats to date, each under the name Spiritual Practices for the Active Work Life. These retreats include experience with particular contemplative practices as well as discussion about the issues we face in our work life and how spiritual practices might help.

Articles: We continue to produce articles and other written material designed to help people think about work and faith-related issues. Most of these are available for reprinting by other groups with proper attribution.

Speaking and Consulting Services: The CFE can provide speakers and consulting services. If you would like to discuss this further, please contact us at mail@faithandenterprise.org.

More information can be found at faithandenterprise.org:

Contact Information:

Center for Faith and Enterprise
P.O. Box 1098
Sierra Madre, CA 91025

mail@faithandenterprise.org

Website: faithandenterprise.org

Podcast: Faith and Enterprise Podcast

To receive updates:
www.faithandenterprise.org/subscribe